Brent Darnell

International

The People-Profit Connection:

How Emotional Intelligence Can Maximize People Skills and Maximize Your Profits

3rd Edition

By
G. Brent Darnell

Praise for The People-Profit Connection

"Brent's enormously readable book demystifies the concept of emotional intelligence and links people skills and success in the construction industry - in fact, in any industry. A definite "must read".
Lisa Fanto, *Senior Vice President, Corporate and Communication Services, Hardin Construction*

"We believe that relationships are our greatest asset. Brent's book takes this central idea, practically applies the concept of emotional intelligence, and offers real solutions to many industry problems. I would recommend it to any construction professional."
Jim Griffin, *CEO, R.J. Griffin & Company*

"Construction has always been a people business, but the human resource challenges of the new millennium have industry players scrambling like never before to capture and utilize talent. Brent Darnell has produced a great handbook for anyone in the construction industry who wishes to elevate their understanding of the human dimension."
Hank Harris, *President, FMI Corporation*

"Brent's book, The People-Profit Connection, has been well received by our managers; they describe it as "on target" for our industry. We use emotional intelligence concepts to support our talent management work, and this book is particularly helpful in making the ideas practical in their application: better relationships produce better business outcomes."
Dr. Pam Mayer, *Succession & Development Manager, Granite Construction Inc.*

"You hit the nail on the head."
Dr. Wayne Clough, *former President, Georgia Institute of Technology, now Secretary of the Smithsonian Institution.*

"Brent Darnell's book provides a critical link to creating high performing and motivated teams by helping us understand Emotional Intelligence. It will help you to create a climate where you can articulate a shared mission that moves people and, ultimately, create successful projects."
Bruce D'Agostino, *Executive Director, Construction Management Association of America*

"Every developer needs to read this little book. Recognizing that our emotional skills control our behavior, Brent identifies the key to great success – care as much about the needs of your team as your own - it's just too simple to be wrong and it applies to so much more than business."
Lou Conti, VP – *Development, Cousins Properties Incorporated*

"Brent Darnell's book makes a very subtle but dramatic point – emotional intelligence is relevant to performance in every job and any industry! He offers compelling stories and powerful insights. The book is full of ideas for improving individual and organizational performance by tapping the power of emotion."
Kate Cannon, *Emotional Intelligence Pioneer*

"Brent Darnell's book accurately depicts the construction industry's reality and its need to change. More importantly, it identifies the emotional skills required to be successful in changing the industry and provides a direction in which the industry must go. In my opinion, without a focus on emotional intelligence, the industry will continue on a slow decline."
Joe Andronaco, *President, USA Technology Services*

"Brent Darnell breaks down the most complicated part of our business – the human psyche – into useable and quantifiable

steps in The People-Profit Connection. The process of placing people in the right positions, and training employees to enhance their people-skills is simplified by using emotional intelligence. This leads to a Win-Win situation with happier employees and better company margins. What more could anyone ask for?"
Rick Alcala, *Construction Consultant*

"Brent's book is a good example for all the companies that want to be better. It shows in a very understandable way how companies can change just by paying REAL attention to their people, which is the only possible way to be different and to become the best."
Josep Sala i Teixidó, *sales manager Spain, Greece, Latin America, Poggenpohl Möbelwerke GmbH (A member of the Nobia group)*

"Mr. Darnell's book deftly explains the complex psychological factors that govern personal relationships in a simple set of readily understandable layman's terms called "Emotional Intelligence." It shows how improving these people skills at every personnel level affects business performance in intuitively obvious, but often overlooked, ways. I recommend it to anyone interested in smooth, safe, and profitable construction."
Bailey Pope, *AIA, VP Design and Construction, Harold A Dawson Company*

"The book is a gem! Easy to read and understand, practical and hands-on."
Margareta Sjölund, *PhD, founder of Kandidata*

"I believe there is a great deal of substance in the approach to utilizing emotional intelligence as a basis to bring about positive changes in Construction Professionals."
Tracy MacDonald, *Project Director, McCarthy Construction*

THE PEOPLE-PROFIT CONNECTION, HOW EMOTIONAL INTELLIGENCE CAN MAXIMIZE PEOPLE SKILLS AND MAXIMIZE YOUR PROFITS

BDI Publishers · ATLANTA
Copyright © 2004, 2007, and 2011
by G. Brent Darnell

Back cover photo by **MK Coppola**
Cover design and layout by **Tudor Maier**

Other books by G. Brent Darnell:

Relationship Skills for Tough Guys: 12 Steps to Great Relationships

Stress Management, Time Management, and Life Balance for Tough Guys: Creating Success on Your Terms

Communication and Presentation Skills for Tough Guys

The Tao of Emotional Intelligence: 82 Ways to Improve Your Social Competence

The Primal Safety Coloring Book

Big Mama's Country Cookbook: Recipes from the True South

Table of Contents

Dedication

This book is dedicated to my parents:

Bob Darnell,
the builder of bridges between people and places,
who taught me how to get along
with my fellow man,

and Betty Darnell,
the life of the party,
who never met a
stranger.

Acknowledgements

I want to thank my wife, Andrea, for all of her encouragement and support. My appreciation also goes to Kate Cannon for her right-on comments, mentoring, and friendship. Hats off to Diana Durek and all of the folks at Multi-Health Systems, Inc., Margareta Sjölund at Kandidata for introducing me to emotional intelligence, Pat Dunwoody of the Associated Builders and Contractors for all of her early help and validation, Pam Pate, the editing guru, and all of the other kind readers who have given me great suggestions and advice. I also want to extend a big thanks to all of the participants from these courses who have started their journey toward personal mastery. Thanks also go to the individuals and companies who took the leap of faith and embraced this work, especially Lisa Fanto and all of the gracious folks at Hardin Construction. To those companies who have agreed to share their case studies, I am eternally grateful. And finally, a huge thanks to Ed Legum for all of his help in turning this book into a reality.

Foreword to the Third Edition
*By **Gary Draper**, Draper & Associates*

When robots and black boxes build projects, we won't need Brent Darnell's advice anymore. Until then, however, we need to pay close attention to what he has to say. Brent's systematic take on the concept of emotional intelligence is not only worth looking into, it also compels us to explore that mysterious region of the project business: the people jungle. It's gotten too expensive to play ostrich when people problems infect the project team. Brent's approach can help each of us to know that:

- We have a people problem.
- We can isolate the cause of the problem.
- We can help fix the problem.

It's true – people can change, and change for the better. And applying emotional intelligence techniques can facilitate that change.

Brent has three histories going for him:

1. Brent learned his first lessons from his dad, Bob Darnell. Bob was a real leader in the construction business and helped people solve their problems using the personal approach. I know because I learned a lot from Bob, too.

2. Brent's in-the-field experience. He's been immersed in the school of hard knocks.

3. Brent's professional experience in applying emotional intelligence for a multitude of clients. Dig in, and you will gain new insights into getting things done in our people-driven world.

Introduction

"God gave us so many emotions, and so many strong ones. Every human being, even if he is an idiot, is a millionaire in emotions."
Isaac Bashevis Singer

"Above all else, guard your heart, for it affects everything that you do."
Proverbs 4:23 (NLT)

"When the human species has learned to harness emotion, we will be ready to take the next evolutionary step."
Charles Darwin

This book was written specifically for the construction industry, but the more I talked to people outside of the construction industry, the more they confirmed that these issues were applicable to many businesses. This is especially true of service industries where the employees are technically educated or trained, such as engineering, healthcare, legal, information technology, telecommunications, manufacturing, finance, and accounting.

They all have similar problems that relate directly to their collaborative, service-oriented nature and the employees' need to effectively deal with people. By addressing these people issues, organizations can be transformed, become less problematic, and add more to their bottom lines. In fact, if these concepts work for the construction industry, which is generally slow to embrace change, they will work for any industry.

Imagine for a moment a brilliant future for the construction industry where highly respected managers balance their toughness, assertiveness, and independence with highly effective interpersonal skills. Imagine an industry that is completely service-oriented and customer focused, with zero defects and total customer satisfaction. Imagine an industry where there is trust, communication, and teamwork among the owners, construction managers, architects, designers, contractors, subcontractors, vendors, and suppliers.

Imagine an industry where all projects are completed ahead of schedule and well within the budget, where collaborative project delivery is the norm, where employees are respected and encouraged to thrive, where productivity skyrockets, and profit margins increase dramatically. Imagine an industry where sustainable construction is just the way we do business, where the industry's processes not only do no harm, but also contribute to a healthier planet.

Consider the power of communication and teamwork so widespread that project teams love to come to work each morning, where relationships are so strong and concern for others is so pervasive that people look out for each other and working safely is as natural as breathing. Imagine a diverse workplace that draws millions of young men, women, and minorities because they want to be a part of this wonderful business, to work together to build something, to create something from nothing. That is the industry I want to be a part of, that is waiting to be.

But the big question is, "Why isn't the industry like that now?" It's a very good question that deserves an answer. In fact, that is the purpose of this book – to determine how the industry can transform itself into the one I have just described. There are many seemingly unsolvable problems that prevent us from having such an industry. I'm sure you are thinking of those problems right now. The first step toward solving these complex issues is to find their root causes. Once we do that, we can begin to find solutions.

I have asked successful construction people about these industry problems and have heard many different responses, but the common denominator seems to be related to difficulties with people. One person joked, "If it weren't for the people, this would be a fun business." When construction professionals were asked where they spend the majority of their time, they replied, "Dealing with people problems." Ask yourself this question: Are most of your problems process oriented or people oriented? The answer is obvious. We all know that this is a difficult industry made more complicated by the myriad of problems associated with this human dimension, which probably goes back to the building of the pyramids.

The dilemma is that no one has come up with an effective way to solve these people problems – until now. This book explores the most difficult construction industry problems, provides some insight into their root causes, and shows how to go about solving them. And when your company solves these problems, your bottom line will dramatically increase. In order to address people issues, it is logical that we examine the people. That is where emotional intelligence comes in.

What is emotional intelligence? One simple definition is "social competence". By cultivating a high level of personal mastery, you are able to deal more effectively with others. This can be a difficult but worthwhile process. As Lao Tzu said, "Mastering others is strength. Mastering yourself makes you fearless." Using emotional intelligence as a foundation, we have found a way to measure and improve people skills and solve people-related problems. Teaching people skills to contractors and engineers using emotional intelligence is the basis of our business.

At the beginning of this journey, when I told my wife I was going to teach emotional intelligence to contractors and engineers, she said I was crazy. How in the world could I teach these tough construction managers about emotional intelligence? Even I had my doubts. How would they react to learning about their own emotions and the emotions of others? The initial reactions, which are now predictable, were apprehension, skepticism, and resistance. But once these initial reactions were overcome, and participants realized that emotional intelligence was something that could be quite important for their career development and personal lives, virtually all of them embraced the concept. And once they embraced the concept and worked on their emotional intelligence, the results were nothing short of remarkable.

As one participant put it, "I was apprehensive about this type of training in the beginning. However, after completing the course and seeing my own personal growth, I realize that the effort given has netted significant results." Another participant said, "There were times when I felt like the Karate Kid. I kept asking myself, 'why am I continuing to 'wax on, wax off'?' But in the end, the lessons really paid off." Another participant put it this way: "In the beginning I was a bit skeptical of how much the program could help but after some honest soul searching and opening my mind to some unconventional (for a construction guy) techniques, some big changes were made. The program along with some diet alterations helped me change some long standing problems that has helped me tremendously with my life and career." A Senior Vice President for a top 200 contractor said, "When you came in to talk to me about this approach to management training, I was intensely skeptical. But overall, I don't think you can get through the classes without greater awareness. And that awareness leads to behavioral change. We see that on the back end with how we manage our people, turnover numbers, and morale." By the way, it seems that 75% of our testimonials begin with "I was skeptical in the beginning."

This focus on the people side of business is nothing new. The introduction to Dale Carnegie's *How to Win Friends and Influence People*, which was published in 1936, states: "Research done a few years ago under the auspices of the Carnegie Foundation for the Advancement of Teaching uncovered a most important and significant fact – a fact later confirmed by additional studies made at the Carnegie Institute of Technology. These investigations revealed that even in such technical lines as engineering, about fifteen percent of one's financial success is due to one's technical knowledge and about eighty-five percent is due to skill in human engineering – to personality and the ability to lead people." (1)

When I first started working with emotional intelligence, my skeptical engineer's brain had many questions. You will likely have similar questions and challenges as well. This book will answer your questions and give you a path to follow. We will discuss the basics of emotional intelligence and why it is vital to your future success and the success of your company. By using the methodology outlined in this book, you will be able to develop and improve your emotional intelligence and make your life better at work and at home. For companies, you will be able to solve the problems that continue to plague your business and increase your bottom line.

There are many free resources available on my website (www. brentdarnell.com) to help you with your journey, including numerous articles, video links, a mini-Emotional Intelligence test, and an Emotional Intelligence workbook so that you can create development plans. When you land on the home page, click on the download center, register and create a profile, and download away! See Appendix A for more information.

CHAPTER 1

An Introduction to Emotional Intelligence

"People do not remember you by any intellectual idea or concept you may have given them, but by some subtle emotional impression you may have made consciously or unconsciously. It is what one thinks about you after you have left him that counts."

Frances Wilshire

What makes a great leader? Think for a moment about a great leader whom you admire, someone you really look up to. What are the characteristics that make this person great? Whenever I ask this question, I usually get a long list of skills. A great leader has good communication skills, empathy, listening skills, passion, assertiveness, focus, decisiveness, motivation skills, relationship skills, and vision. Invariably, it is a long list of the so-called "soft" skills, or emotional intelligence competencies. Very rarely does anyone say that a great leader has incredible technical skill or vast intellect or an advanced degree from a prestigious college.

Isn't this list of attributes just as valid for most areas of the construction business? Think of the best owner's representative, the best architect, the best designer, the best construction manager, the best laborer, the best carpenter, the best plumber, the best electrician, the best superintendent, or the best project manager. Don't most of them possess good people skills? Aren't these people skills a vital part of what makes them effective and what makes you want to work with them? Don't we continually receive requests for our best people, the ones who have those great interpersonal skills? Isn't it a shame that we can't put them on all of our projects? If people skills differentiate these stars, then why don't we try to cultivate these skills in all of our employees?

Our decisions are based on emotional responses. The choices we make, the red Mustang, the dark woman with red hair, that favorite pair of blue jeans, even something as simple as how you like your eggs are triggered by emotional impulses. In fact, recent brain research reveals that the emotional part of the brain is involved in every aspect of our day-to-day thought processes. Without this connection to the emotional part of the brain, cognitive thought processes such as decision making are impossible.

Even information that we perceive with our senses is filtered through the emotional part of our brains, coloring it with our perceptions, our past experiences, and values. Because of the way we process this information, we do, truly, create our own reality. There is a story of a family that was thinking of moving to a new town. They stopped at the local gas station in the prospective town and asked the attendant about the people there. They asked him what kind of people they were. The gas station attendant asked them what the people were like in the town that they had left. They told the attendant that the people in their former town were mean, petty, and selfish and that was the reason they were leaving. He told them that the people in the prospective town were exactly the same: mean, petty, and selfish. The family drove off to the next town in search of a new place to live. The attendant knew that the family created that reality, and it would be the same no matter where they moved.

I have a personal story about how emotional energy, specifically optimism, created a desired outcome. The main thing we teach is how to manage your emotions for the best outcomes. I am known to be overly optimistic. I score high in optimism and low in reality testing. My wife calls me "optimistic to the point of ridiculous". I was in Sweden teaching a course for a week. Keep in mind we were out in the middle of nowhere right on the Baltic Sea. On Monday evening, after a nice sauna, I jumped into the Baltic, which was around forty-five degrees, and lost my glasses. I didn't have a backup pair of glasses or a pair of contacts. This was a disaster. I couldn't see the screen to teach and had a hard time conducting the training sessions.

I called my wife and told her that I was going to find a glasses place, and I could look into a machine, and then they would give me my new glasses. She said she didn't think they could do that, but I was undaunted. Just in case, she contacted my optometrist and had my glasses prescription faxed to the conference center. In the meantime, I told my wife that I would try to find someone with a diving mask or goggles so that I could dive down into the forty-five degree water and find my glasses. But without my glasses, I'm not sure I could see well enough to find them. But I was undaunted. My wife thought this was ridiculous on two levels. One, we were in Sweden. Who is going to have diving equipment? Two, the Baltic has tides. There is no way those glasses are going to be there after several days. But I was undaunted.

I talked to the bartender at the conference center, who told me that she just returned from a diving trip in Egypt and had a pair of diving goggles. She said that there was a small glasses boutique in the village where I might be able to get some contacts. And if I had contacts, I could use the goggles, dive down into the forty-five degree water and find my glasses. Keep in mind that time is passing. It is Wednesday now. I managed in the classroom, but could not drive into the village on Wednesday because of something we had to do as a class that evening. I went to the

glasses boutique with my prescription on Thursday afternoon.
Of course, they can't give you glasses by looking into a machine.
This place didn't even have a machine to look into. But they did
have contacts for me. So Thursday evening, I went back to the
conference center with my contacts in and the diving goggles
in hand. But it was too dark to look that night. I would have to
wait until Friday.

Friday morning came, and I put on my bathing suit, my contacts,
and my goggles. All of the participants were seated on the deck
overlooking the sea, waiting for the bus. They all told me it was
a waste of time and that after four days, the glasses would be
impossible to find. I dove into the forty-five degree water. It
took my breath, but I swam down about twelve feet and there
they were. My glasses half buried in the sand. I picked them up
and triumphantly broke the surface of the water, holding
them high over my head. The participants thought I had
staged the whole thing to teach them a lesson about
optimism and creating outcomes.

Did managing my emotions and staying optimistic affect the
outcome of this situation? I'm sure that it did. By staying focused
on the desired outcome despite what logic and common sense
told me, the outcome was a positive one. I believe that I actually
created that reality and affected that outcome by what I chose
to think and feel. Imagine the power of this in your day-to-day
encounters with life's challenging situations.

The latest neuroscience bears this phenomenon out. The way
we view reality is based on emotional responses, no matter
how objective we think we are being. That is the reason
that "eyewitness" testimony can be very unreliable. If five
witnesses experience the same event, you will likely get five
different stories. Think of the consequences of this reality on
a construction project. Think of the number of realities that
must be reconciled in order to bring a project to a successful
conclusion.

Simply put, our brains are hardwired for emotion. We can't escape it. The limbic system, or the primitive, emotional center of our brain, is working all of the time. There is an interesting case study in the book, *Emotional Intelligence*, by Daniel Goleman, a leader in this field. He tells us about Elliot, a successful lawyer, whose brain was damaged during an operation. The area that was damaged was the part of the brain that links the emotional part to the thinking part. Although he was cognitively intelligent, because he could not call upon the emotional part of his brain, he functioned more like a computer.

As a result, his life fell apart. "He could no longer hold a job. His wife left him. Squandering his savings on fruitless investments, he was reduced to living in a spare bedroom in his brother's home." (2) Without this emotional link, the thinking brain could no longer assign values to the situations that arose. According to Goleman, "every option was neutral".

We also have something in our brains called mirror neurons. These neurons mirror the emotions of the person sitting across from us. In short, emotions create energy and energy affects outcomes whether you are aware of it or not. Have you ever walked into a room and thought that the tension was so thick you could cut it with a knife? This is that emotional energy you are picking up on. When we say that emotions are contagious, it's actually true from a physiological standpoint. At the beginning of our first Total Leadership Program, we demonstrated this phenomenon. We sent Jonelle, our Executive Assistant, out of the room and told the participants that when I gave them the thumbs up, they were to think positive thoughts about Jonelle. When I gave them the thumbs down, they were to think negative thoughts about her.

She came back in, and we blindfolded her so she could not pick up on body language or facial cues. We sat her down and we performed kinesiology (muscle testing) on her. Basically, Jonelle held her arm out and tried to resist when Dr. Robbins, our resident kinesiologist, pushed it down. If she stayed strong, it meant that whatever she was experiencing was beneficial to her body. If she went weak, it meant that whatever she was experiencing was detrimental to her body. I started with thumbs up. She received positive thoughts from the group. She went strong. Then I did thumbs down. She received negative thoughts from the group. She went weak. I did thumbs up again. She went strong. After this, we heard someone from the audience say, "That's bullshit."

It was David, the COO of a glass installation company. David is a big, tough guy, a Marine, and a skeptical, no-nonsense person. His boss was kind enough to push him to the front of the room and said, "You try it." So, David came up in his camouflage ball cap, and we sat him down. Since he had seen the exercise, we decided to do a verbal version of it. Dr. Robbins tested him. He was quite strong, and David is a big guy. Keep in mind that Dr. Robbins is 5' 2" and weighs only 107 pounds. I told David all things positive, that he was a valued employee, that he was a great guy, great dad, great employee. His arm stayed strong. No matter how hard Dr. Robbins tried, she couldn't get his arm to go down.

Then, we went negative. I said, "David, you're a worthless piece of crap. I don't like you. I've never liked you. You're a horrible father. You're destroying your kid's lives." His arm went down easily. In fact, Dr. Robbins pushed it down with one finger. Then we went back to positive so as not to leave David with all of that negativity. David was a little shaken. We saw him later that evening and he told us, "There was no way in hell I was gonna let that little woman push my arm down." He further said that whatever we told him, he was just going to believe it. If you want to see the video of this entire episode, it is available in our download center. Go to *www.brentdarnell.com*, download center, video links, and David's revelation about emotions. Then you can go to his interview afterward under video interviews: Interview with David.

David had the typical alpha male profile, but the Total Leadership Program changed his life and opened up opportunities for him. He was going through a rough time personally with custody battles, long commutes, and children with health issues. He attributes the program with helping him to deal with these highly emotional and stressful issues and maintaining peak performance both mentally and physically. It also opened up opportunities for him at work. He is taking on more responsibility for the operations and leadership at his company.

The people who study emotional intelligence began by asking a very simple, but profound question: What makes people successful? They tried to quantify it. They looked at IQ and other intelligence indicators. They looked at higher learning and technical training. Did success lie in having the best education? What about MBAs, PhDs and other postgraduate degrees? Did they give people the competitive edge to become more successful?

Of course, the other thing that we need to define is "success". We could come up with a thousand definitions. Is it based on social function, financial success, peer approval, a level of happiness? For the purpose of this book, we will try to simplify things. Let's define success as being a top performer in your field.

So, who are the most successful people? The answer probably won't surprise you. It isn't the people with the highest IQs or the people with the highest levels of technical or academic ability. Many of the most successful people have average IQs and education levels. So if it isn't technical skill, higher education, or intellectual intelligence, what makes people successful?

According to David Caruso, another leader in the field of emotional intelligence, most successful people have learned to "accurately identify emotions, use these emotions to influence how [they] think, understand the underlying causes of these emotions, and manage with emotions by integrating the wisdom of these feelings into [their] thinking." (3) Beyond that, most successful people have learned to understand emotions in others and make true emotional connections. According to Irwin Federman, a partner at US Venture Partners, great leaders know that "people will work harder for someone they like, and they like you in direct proportion to the way you make them feel."

All things being equal, the people who excel are the ones with higher levels of emotional intelligence. Not that technical ability is unimportant. In fact, it is important for success, especially in the construction industry. But technical ability and experience can only take you so far. One construction leader called it "the price of entry", but once that technical knowledge is in place, emotional intelligence is vital for ongoing success. One program participant put it this way, "Relationships and impressions are just as important as bricks and mortar."

The following is a graphical representation of the emotional intelligence and knowledge axes. For the purposes of this book, we will use "construction manager" as a generic term to include anyone who is involved in managing the various parts of the construction process. These managers tend to have medium to high levels of specialized knowledge, but average to low emotional intelligence and even lower interpersonal skills.

HIGH EMOTIONAL INTELLIGENCE	
steady performer	high performers
moderate to high success	high success
may hit career limit	good life/work balance
great relationships	low stress
moderate to high happiness	high happiness
medium to high stress	self development
	great relationships
LOW KNOWLEDGE (education, cognitive learning/tech ability)	**HIGH KNOWLEDGE** (education, cognitive learning/tech ability)
low performers	technically trained
inability to maintain relationships	PhD's, researchers
inability to maintain jobs	engineers
unhappy	can't deal w/people
high stress	poor relationships
blames others	medium to high stress
LOW EMOTIONAL INTELLIGENCE	

Most construction folks tend to be in the highlighted box. The technically educated people in the construction industry such as civil engineers and building construction majors receive very little "people skills" training while in school. There are few courses on interpersonal relationships, communication, empathy, or teamwork. I have also investigated the curricula of several MBA programs, and most of those programs do not cover these areas in any depth. It is a fundamental flaw in our education system, especially for technical people.

Several schools are aware of this deficit and are taking decisive action. They understand that although they are providing an excellent technical education to their students, they are not properly preparing them for the real world, where relationships are a vital key to their success. I am now working with the Architectural Engineering Department at Penn State, the College of Architecture, Design, and Construction at Auburn University, and the Building Construction Department at Virginia Tech. At Penn State, we are working to create an online course on emotional intelligence using this book as a textbook so that students will have a better chance for success. This can be a difficult sell to faculty members at these technical institutions, but they are starting to realize that technical knowledge will only get their graduates so far.

Parker J. Palmer, in his book, *The Courage to Teach*, puts it this way: "If we are to educate a new professional, we must take our students' emotional intelligence as seriously as we take their cognitive intelligence. We must do more than affirm and harness the power of emotions to animate both learning and leadership. If students are to learn and lead well, we must help them develop the skill of 'mining' their emotions for knowledge."

On the field side, those who come up through the field under a mentor with good people skills will have a greater tendency to use these skills. But if they came up under one of those "old school" managers, they may be using the old "kick ass and take names" style to their own detriment. Managers who focus on these non-technical skills and embrace emotional intelligence become better leaders. One program participant said, "Improving my emotional intelligence built up my self-confidence and optimism. I started to think and act a lot more using emotional intelligence. We have stressful situations in my business unit and this has helped me to take my company through the hard times."

These leaders have learned to tap into that very important part of themselves. They have discovered that they can measure and improve these "soft skills", change behaviors, and increase performance. They become more effective both personally and professionally. There are dozens of testimonials documenting improvements in leadership skills and people skills as a result of this work with emotional intelligence. Visit my website *www.brentdarnell.com* for case studies of companies and testimonials of managers who have enhanced their emotional intelligence, increased their effectiveness, and improved the way they work.

There are several instruments that measure emotional intelligence. The most widely used instruments for measuring emotional intelligence is the Bar-On Emotional Quotient Inventory, or EQ-i®. This evaluation was seventeen years in development, and there are over 1,000,000 evaluations in the database. Reuven Bar-On coined the term "EQ" (Emotional Quotient) to represent emotional competence as opposed to IQ (Intellectual Quotient), which measures intellectual capacity.

The Bar-On EQ-i® is a validated, self-perception instrument that measures five main scales (intrapersonal, interpersonal, stress management, adaptability, and general mood). Within each of these scales, there are individual competencies or subscales. Here are the definitions of each of these competencies:

INTRAPERSONAL:

Self-Regard is the ability to respect and accept oneself as basically good. It is also related to self-confidence.

Emotional Self-Awareness is the ability to recognize one's feelings and share them appropriately with others.

Assertiveness is the ability to express feelings, beliefs and thoughts and defend one's rights in a non-destructive manner.

Independence is the ability to be self-directed and self-controlled in one's thinking and actions and to be free from emotional dependency.

Self-Actualization is the ability to realize ones potential, using your talents to the best of your ability, to be generally satisfied with your life.

INTERPERSONAL:

Empathy is the ability to be aware of, to understand, and to appreciate the feelings of others. (Note: This is not to be confused with sympathy, which is feeling sorry for the other person.)

Social Responsibility is the ability to demonstrate oneself as a cooperative, contributing, and constructive member of a larger group.

Interpersonal Relationships is the ability to establish and maintain mutually satisfying relationships.

STRESS MANAGEMENT:

Stress Tolerance is the ability to withstand adverse events and stressful situations without "falling apart" by actively and positively coping with stress.

Impulse Control is the ability to resist or delay an impulse, drive, or temptation to act.

ADAPTABILITY:

Reality Testing is the ability to see the real situation and not be overly optimistic or pessimistic.

Flexibility is the ability to adjust one's emotions, thoughts and behavior to changing situations and conditions.

Problem Solving is the ability to identify and solve problems as well as to generate and implement potentially effective solutions.

GENERAL MOOD:

Optimism is the ability to look at the brighter side of life and to maintain a positive attitude, even in the face of adversity.

Happiness is the ability to feel satisfied with one's life, to enjoy yourself and others, and to have fun.

When this EQ-i® evaluation is taken, the results are compared against a normative group, or a large group of people who have taken the evaluation. The numerical results for each competency fall into a bell curve. Similar to an IQ test, 100 is the mean or average. Scores ranging from 90-110 are considered average or adequate emotional functioning. Scores higher or lower than this range can indicate that the respondent is above or below average.

By measuring these fifteen competencies and more importantly, by comparing the relationships among them, we can determine problem areas to target for improvement. Hundreds of people in the construction industry have taken this evaluation and not one has said that the results were invalid. In fact, almost all of the people to whom we have given feedback have agreed that the evaluation was quite accurate. The validity scales that are built into the evaluation bear this out as they are usually well within the normal range. I believe it is because of the technical participants' desire to be accurate. They want the results to reflect their behavior.

Occasionally, a respondent will tell us that they think some of their low scores, such as empathy or interpersonal relationship skills, are inaccurate. First of all, we point out that it is a self-perception evaluation. The computer spits out what you put in. We also point out that these scores are relative scores to the general population normative group. When this happens, we ask them to show the results to the people who know them well, such as their spouse or close friend or colleague. Each time they have returned and told us that these other people agree with their EQ-i® results indicating that they probably do need to work on those particular skills.

After seeing hundreds of these EQ profiles for construction folks, a definite pattern emerged. Although there were individual differences, every group with whom we worked had virtually the same EQ profile. We have aggregated all of the scores from almost 500 construction managers into a group EQ profile for the construction industry. This group includes over fifty different companies from all over the world and a wide cross section of people from various parts of the construction industry including general contractors, subcontractors, vendors, suppliers, construction managers, design firms, and architectural firms. The positions include assistant superintendents, superintendents, assistant project managers, project managers, senior project managers, subcontractor owners and employees, architects, engineers, building construction majors, business unit managers, estimators, sales people, production people, vice presidents, senior vice presidents, business developers, project executives, COOs, CEOs, CFOs, and a small number of support folks such as accountants, marketing staff, human resource, and information technology people. Although most of the participants were men, there were a few women.

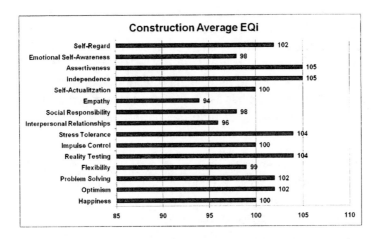

The first thing that stands out is a relatively low score in emotional self-awareness, which is key for good emotional management. Also note the relatively high assertiveness, independence, and self-regard (above the mean) in contrast to lower scores on interpersonal skills across the board (low empathy, low social responsibility, and low interpersonal relationship skills). All of these are below the mean. Keep in mind that this is an average profile. Some of the participants scored quite high in interpersonal skills, making the average higher. We have worked with some participants whose interpersonal scores were in the 50s. Look at it this way, a group of almost 500 technical people couldn't get empathy or interpersonal relationship skills to the mean. Low scores in the areas of emotional self-awareness, empathy, and interpersonal relationships are so pervasive, we call it "the trinity". Many industry professionals we work with choose to develop these three competencies.

More importantly, with a differential of eleven points between assertiveness and empathy, five points between assertiveness and impulse control, seven points between independence and social responsibility, most construction managers will be perceived as aggressive, independent, and capable, but many will come across as impulsive people who don't listen well, seldom ask for input from others, won't involve others in decision making processes, and are often blunt and undiplomatic. They also have a tendency toward the control/perfectionist profile (high problem solving and reality testing along with low flexibility). This group has a need for control and getting things "right". They have a hard time delegating and a tendency to micromanage.

This group also tends to have high stress tolerance and low impulse control. This is a chaos profile based on a reactive management style, which is inherent in the industry. Most managers go from crisis to crisis. Due to this crisis management style, they usually spend little time developing themselves or mentoring subordinates. Although people with this profile can handle a lot of stress, we have found that many exhibit physical symptoms of stress like fatigue, difficulty sleeping, pain, stomach problems, headaches, and irritability.

This group scores relatively high in reality testing, which means that they are neither overly optimistic nor pessimistic and usually see things in black and white. In other words, there is a right way and a wrong way to do things. In addition, the self-actualization and happiness scores for this group tend to be relatively low. This speaks volumes about the industry today. Many believe that it just isn't as fun as it used to be. And with the recent economic downturn, we have seen happiness and optimism trending down.

Also, note that without the strong interpersonal skills to balance competencies like assertiveness, independence, and self-regard, these strengths can become weaknesses. Someone with high assertiveness can become aggressive, someone with high independence can become a loner who doesn't interact with others, and someone with high self-regard can become arrogant.

Prior to the publication of the first edition of this book, Brian

K. Walker of Virginia Polytechnic Institute and State University wrote his Master's Thesis titled Emotional Intelligence Within the A/E/C Industry: A Step Toward Effective Collaboration (May 28, 2003). Mr. Walker's statistical analysis of 104 total participants from seven different companies revealed a typical construction person profile that was almost identical to mine. This data is further evidence of this typical construction manager EQ profile, which seems to be consistent across the industry.

There are other EQ profiles that can indicate performance or behavioral issues. A low score on assertiveness, independence, and self-regard, along with relatively high scores on empathy and social responsibility may indicate a person who has trouble saying no, who gets taken advantage of or walked on. These people may have trouble negotiating and firmly stating their beliefs. This profile is rare in construction managers, but more common for administrative and support positions. It would be very beneficial to know about this profile prior to hiring because this can be problematic for supervisory positions. We've all seen those poor souls who just can't seem to stand up for themselves, but by working on their assertiveness, independence, and self-regard, they can become much more effective.

Low self-actualization along with low happiness and optimism in a forty-plus-year-old may indicate the proverbial mid-life crisis, which could affect productivity at work. Many participants with this profile admit that they are questioning their direction in life and are not satisfied with where they are. If we can identify this situation early, we can make positive changes before they buy that Harley motorcycle and leave the company to go on a cross-country road trip.

This same profile is typical for new parents, especially when the score for social responsibility is also low. You've seen the new father, bleary-eyed and exhausted for the first few months of the baby's life. This certainly affects his productivity at work. Both of these issues can be addressed by working on a clear direction for the employee's life and career and letting them know that this is just a transitory period in their lives.

If we see low self-actualization, stress tolerance, optimism, and happiness, this is a burnout profile. Stress and burnout are huge issues in the industry, and the cost is high in both business and human terms. The statistics on the increase in stress and burnout are alarming. You see these people all of the time in the industry. They are overweight and out of shape, with poor eating habits and dysfunctional lifestyles. They feel trapped and are caught in the downward spiral to poor health. They work too much, eat poorly, and don't exercise, which makes them less efficient mentally and physically. Then, they have to work more and have even less energy left for exercise. This usually goes on until there is a health crisis such as a heart attack or stress-related illness.

Accurate evaluation and early identification of stress and burnout along with lifestyle adjustments, proper nutrition, exercise, and stress reduction can prevent problems such as absenteeism, low productivity, and stress-related illnesses.

High assertiveness, low impulse control, and low flexibility may indicate a problem with anger management or other impulsive behavior. You've seen the guy who storms into the jobsite trailer, yelling and swearing and throwing his hard hat. It's not a pretty sight. By working on these fundamental emotional competencies, managers are better able to control angry outbursts and work toward a fundamental change in behavior. This makes them much more effective in their dealings with project stakeholders. Another pairing of competencies that indicates a particular behavior: high flexibility and low impulse control. These are people who are a little on the ADHD side, starting many projects but rarely finishing them. They tend to float from task to task and have poor time management skills. They also tend to be Crackberry addicts. They can't resist checking their emails constantly.

For the construction industry, there are several advantages to focusing on emotional intelligence as a way to develop people and solve industry problems:

1. Many companies realize the importance of "soft skills" and invest in the training of these skills, but rarely know if the training has been effective. This is a way to measure and improve these skills to produce tangible, fundamental changes in behavior.

2. Emotional intelligence work may answer previously unanswered questions for individuals in your company. Employees may already know that they have difficulty with relationships or anger management problems. They may have been told during their review process that they need to "work on their people skills" or "be nicer to people". The problem is that they may not be able to pinpoint exactly how to do that. But once they take the EQ-i® evaluation and see low scores on empathy or impulse control, they are able to focus on these specific areas to create fundamental behavioral change.

3. Engineers and technically educated or trained people like numbers. As construction people, we are obsessed with them – tolerances, schedules, budget numbers, manpower, productivity numbers, etc. Most construction folks are not shy about sharing their scores. They boast of high scores and sheepishly share their low scores (usually in the interpersonal skills) and vow that they will increase them. People in the industry are much more likely to embrace this work because it produces tangible results that can be measured and improved.

In fact, many practitioners who work with Fortune 500 companies wonder why the results are so good with our programs. Part of the reason is that the people in the construction industry are results driven. Once they see the value of this work, they attack it like they attack a tough project. They do the work necessary to create behavioral change. And these changes show up as statistically significant increases in their EQ-i® scores. There are many case studies available from my website. See Appendix A for more information.

Emotional intelligence is imperative for effective performance. If we evaluate our employees' emotional competencies, identify their developmental needs, and help them to work on these areas, they will improve these skills, increase their effectiveness, and eventually contribute more to the bottom line.

CHAPTER 2

Emotional Intelligence and the Bottom Line

"People work for people, not companies. A worker's regard for his supervisor will affect his opinion of his employer. Production is related to attitude, so much so that an organization which disregards this human equation will not achieve as much as it could achieve".

Gerard R. Griffin

We talked in chapter one about the "old school" construction manager. For those of us who have been in the construction industry for a while, we all know who the "old school" construction manager is. He's the one who kicks ass and takes names, the one who gets the job done. He doesn't take crap from anybody, punishes subcontractors, and holds the owner's and the architect's feet to the fire. He doesn't think twice about compromising safety if he thinks it will increase his profit and personal bonus. If he is working on a hard bid project, he finds a large percentage of change orders due to errors and omissions in the drawings, specifications, and contracts. He is willing to make others look bad so that his company can look good. It is his philosophy that since the next project will probably be awarded to the low bidder, it is unnecessary to create and maintain good relationships. It is far more important to "win" at all costs.

But the face of construction is changing. The industry is becoming more of a service industry. We are getting away from the notion of delivering a building to an owner and walking away. We are seeing more design-build and negotiated projects, more integrated project delivery, more team approaches beyond mere partnering agreements, more ongoing service contracts, and more repeat business. This "old school" guy is becoming a dinosaur.

The new construction manager not only needs high levels of assertiveness, self-regard, and independence, but it would benefit him to have balance in his emotional makeup. With this balance, he would be more likeable, with strong empathy, communication, and relationship skills. He would be able to build teams and carry out a project plan with a sense of cooperation, constantly looking for "win-win" outcomes. One participant put it this way, "It is not what you know, but the way you present things. Leading and motivating is not just pointing and screaming."

Balfour Beatty is one of the top contractors in the USA. According to John Tarpey, the Division President and CEO for Balfour Beatty in Washington, DC, there are four basic areas of product delivery for the construction industry: schedule, budget, quality, and relationships. Most contractors are fairly adept at the first three, but it is the last area, the area of relationships, where many contractors fail. Ask yourself what a client remembers a year after a project is complete. Is it that the project was built on time, within a budget with reasonable quality? More likely what will be remembered are the relationships on the project-good or bad.

The following chart is an EQ profile for a forty-seven year old high school educated man who owns a highly successful contracting business.

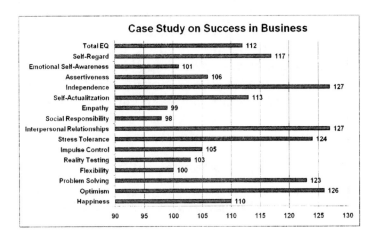

Case Study on Success in Business

His EQ-i® results may explain why he has done so well. This person's total EQ score was close to the upper limits of the average range (112), which suggests that he was well prepared to deal with the usual demands and pressures of everyday life. By studying six of his highest scores, it became quite clear how he became so successful. His intrapersonal strength stems from his positive self-regard (SR=117) and a very high degree of independence (IN=127). Moreover, one of his highest scores was in the interpersonal relationship domain (IR=127). These intrapersonal and interpersonal strengths combine with a very high degree of optimism (OP=126), stress tolerance (ST=124), and a down-to-earth, highly developed ability to solve problems (PS=123).

Other people considered him to be a "very good person to work with and for." Interestingly, he received a total IQ score of 102 on an intelligence test that was given toward the end of his last year in high school. An IQ of 102 placed his cognitive intelligence in the middle of the average range; his grades in high school were also average.

Although he had some of the typical construction manager traits such as relatively lower empathy and flexibility, along with higher self-regard and independence, this guy is great with relationships. There is still work to do to create a more balanced profile. I would start with emotional self-awareness, empathy, and flexibility. But even without a more balanced profile, he has used his emotional intelligence, especially his interpersonal skills, to his advantage. This has thoroughly prepared him for the paradigm shifts in the construction industry.

Let's take a closer look at some of these shifts:

Old Paradigm	New Paradigm
Large labor pool	Competition for talent
Homogenous, male dominated labor pool	Multi-cultural labor pool with more females
Baby boomer workforce	Multi-generational workforce
Manage processes	Manage people
Low bid work	Negotiated work
Short, adversarial relationships	Long, satisfying relationships
Projects run from silos	Integrated project delivery systems
Lack of client focus	Focus on client and his needs
Communication lacking	Communication focus
Decrease overhead	Increase performance
Safety a nuisance	Focus on safety
Environmental ignorance	Environmental focus
High stress/burnout	Focus to reduce stress/burnout

This new paradigm requires a different set of skills than the old paradigm. The problem is that the typical emotional intelligence profile for construction folks is in direct contrast to the skills required for this shift. Let's revisit the typical construction industry EQ profile found in Chapter 1. In an industry where collaboration, good relationships, teamwork, flexibility, and communication are essential for success, the people who are attracted to this business generally have low emotional self-awareness (lack of understanding of self), high assertiveness (aggressiveness), high independence (not a team player), high self-regard (sometimes approaching arrogance), low empathy (lack of understanding of others), low social responsibility (they don't work well in groups), and low interpersonal relationship skills. The data is consistent and undeniable. Think about it. Many of the people in the construction industry have this typical profile. No wonder it's such a difficult business!

Emotional intelligence is not some "touchy-feely" approach to management. It's not about group hugs and everyone getting along like robots. As we said before, we are hardwired for emotion, and it is integral to the way we think and interact with people. Understanding others helps us to be more effective. Peter, one of our participants put it this way, "I've learned that being able to understand what is motivating the other parties is essential for achieving your objectives." Another participant called this understanding "a definite competitive advantage". But with this typical EQ profile, understanding others is limited.

How many people can you think of in the construction industry with this typical EQ profile? How many employees has your company given up on because of their lack of people skills? Now there is hope for these people. By evaluating and improving their emotional intelligence, they will be able to thrive in this new paradigm.

Most companies are not prepared for these industry shifts, nor do they know how to cope with them. But the key to dealing with these shifts is in addressing the emotional intelligence needs of your employees and your company. In fact, it is critical for your future success. You must give your employees the proper tools, training, and encouragement to survive in this changing climate in the construction industry. You must pay attention to their emotional competencies, evaluate them, identify developmental needs, and provide programs that will enhance their social competence. Without these skills, without the proper emotional tools, managers will fail in this new work environment.

Companies who ignore these trends will lose work, lose employees, reduce their margins, and eventually go out of business. But those companies who pay attention to this vital work will hire great people, help them with their emotional development, create lasting client and stakeholder relationships, and thrive in this new marketplace, ultimately adding a great deal to the bottom line.

Industry Problems

"You can't win without being completely different. When everyone else says we're crazy, I say, 'Gee, we must really be onto something.'"
Larry Ellison, Founder of Oracle

"Innovation is more than a new method. It is a new view of the universe, as one of risk rather than of chance or of certainty. It is a new view of man's role in the universe; he creates order by taking risks. And this means that innovation, rather than being an assertion of human power, is an acceptance of human responsibility."
Peter Drucker

"You can't invent the transistor by trying to perfect the vacuum tube."
Sign at Bell Labs

Introduction:

We are now going to delve into some of the more pressing issues in the construction industry. But these issues are not limited to the construction industry. I'm sure you will recognize that these are problems in many businesses, especially those in technical industries. We will focus on probable causes, potential solutions, and how they affect the bottom line. The root cause of many of the industry problems is due to the typical emotional intelligence profile for construction managers. If we can address these areas and create fundamental change in our people, it will have a profound effect on the entire industry.

CHAPTER 3

SAFETY ISSUES

Anyone who has ever been on a project where there was a serious accident knows that horrible feeling in the pit of your stomach when the radio crackles with the news that someone has been badly injured or killed, and you hear the siren of an ambulance in the distance. No matter how successful the project is, that is the one thing that will always be remembered.

Safety is a huge issue. Not only is there a moral imperative to improve safety, but accidents and other safety issues cost the industry billions of dollars per year in high insurance costs, lawsuits, Occupational Health and Safety Administration (OSHA) fines, and image problems. We all know that construction is a hazardous occupation. In the United States, during the period from 1980 through 1995, at least 17,000 construction workers died from injuries suffered on the job. Can you imagine what these statistics are worldwide?

In the United States, construction lost more workers to death from traumatic injury than any other major industrial sector during this time period. Construction has the third highest rate of death by injury: 15.2 deaths per 100,000 workers. This figure for 2005 dropped to 11 deaths per 100,000 workers, but it is still high. Only mining and agriculture experience higher rates. According to the Bureau of Labor Statistics, in 2007, construction had the most deaths of any private sector industry with 1,178. The leading causes of death among construction workers are falls from elevations, motor vehicle crashes, electrocution, machine accidents, and being struck by falling objects. (4)

What is the problem? Do people want to work unsafely? If you ask them this question, their answer is a resounding "NO!" When you ask top managers if they want their people to work unsafely, they answer, "Of course not!" So what is the problem here? The present system to ensure project safety is a command and control approach where strict safety rules are implemented. If the rules are not followed, the offending employee is reprimanded or fired. This approach has been marginally successful, but because we have only focused on the objective side of safety, we have reached the limit of its success. To achieve the next level, we must tap into the subjective side and use emotional intelligence.

A contractor had five elevator workers that were not working safely. They were not tying off as they should. The superintendent called them into the trailer and had a talk with them. He sent them home and told them to get a letter from their wives saying that it was okay for them to work unsafely. As soon as he had those letters in his hands, they could go back to work. The elevator guys were a little stunned, and sheepishly went home early. The next day, four of the wives visited the project, and the other one called. They told the superintendent that their husbands had a responsibility to their families to come home alive and unhurt each day, and if their husbands were not working safely to please call them, and they would straighten that situation out in very short order. This is a great use of emotional intelligence with regard to safety.

When you think about it, every person on every project has loved ones – a family, a spouse, a partner, a friend, a child, a brother, a sister, a mother, or a father. When you look at safety from this highly personal perspective and make the emotional connections, when you put it in those personal terms, safety becomes much more than rules and regulations. Specifically, social responsibility, interpersonal relationships, and empathy skills are the keys to a safer work environment. But it all starts with emotional self-awareness. When everyone is aware moment to moment of their surroundings and are able to discern when they are too tired or too stressed to work safely, then you take safety to a whole new level.

There is a popular video making the rounds these days called "Remember Charlie" (www.charliemorecraft.com) in which Charlie Morecraft tells the story of his horrific accident. Charlie didn't follow safety procedures or wear the correct personal protective equipment. The result was a massive fire at a refinery that could have been avoided. Charlie was burned over 50% of his body and took five years out of his life to heal. The film depicts how his injury and recovery almost destroyed his life, and how it affected his family.

His father had a stroke shortly after the accident, he and his wife divorced, and both of his daughters missed having a "daddy" around while they were growing up. He tells of the agony his mother faced each day having to watch him go through the extreme pain of "debridement", a procedure in which the dead skin from the burns is removed in large chlorine tubs.

Even the most hard-hearted superintendent wipes tears away after seeing this video. With an emotionally intelligent approach, safety is no longer a set of rules to begrudgingly follow. There is a paradigm shift. Charlie gives safety a human side.

We have developed a similar video, but it focuses on the construction industry and the injured workers and their families.

It is a powerful way to communicate to others the consequences not only to themselves, but to those who care about them.

Bovis Lend Lease in Atlanta used this type of program with dramatic results. In the United States, insurance companies assign a modifier based on past safety performance. This modifier is called the EMR (Experience Modification Rate). This EMR determines what companies will pay for worker's compensation insurance. The more safely a company works, the lower their EMR. Let's use an example: Say you are buying $100,000 worth of insurance for a project. If your EMR is 1.0 (an EMR of 1.0 is the industry standard), you will pay $100,000 for that insurance. If your EMR is 1.5, you will pay $150,000 for the same insurance. If your EMR is 0.5, you will pay $50,000 for that insurance.

Using an emotionally intelligent approach to safety, Bovis Lend Lease reduced their EMR to 0.34, so they would pay only $34,000 for that insurance. Bovis Lend Lease is not only saving lives and reducing emotional turmoil, but they are saving money and improving their bottom line. Imagine if the entire industry used this approach. The potential cost savings would be staggering, but the potential to decrease human suffering due to death and disability would be even greater.

Let's look at how some other industry issues relate to safety. Communication and teamwork are vital to working safely. Poor communication and ineffective teamwork can contribute to poor safety practices. Controlling stress and burnout can also be a significant factor in preventing accidents. When we are tired or stressed, we have a greater tendency to make mistakes. And mistakes on a construction project can be fatal. We know that when we exercise regularly, eat nutritious foods, and handle our stress, our cognitive abilities are better. Take a look at the typical construction person. He usually has a poor diet, does very little exercise, and is highly stressed. No wonder accidents are pervasive compared to other industries. There is very little focus on these areas, but I believe that improvements in nutrition, exercise, and stress management would create a safer work environment.

And what about alpha males as it relates to safety? There was an article in the July/August 2008 Harvard Business Review called *Unmasking Manly Men* by Robin J. Ely and Debra Meyerson. The article focuses on how roughnecks and roustabouts on oil rigs improved their safety by softening their approach and focusing on the safety and well-being of the workers. According to Ely and Meyerson, "Over the 15-year period these changes in work practices, norms, perceptions, and behaviors were implemented company-wide. The company's accident rate declined by 84% while productivity (number of barrels produced), efficiency (cost per barrel), and reliability (production "up" time) increased beyond the industry's previous benchmark." We have to wonder if this approach was ignored on the Deepwater Horizon oil rig, the site of the worst oil disaster in the history of the industry.

They further state, "If men in the hyper-masculine environment of the oil rigs can let go of the macho ideal and improve their performance, then men in corporate America might be able to do likewise. Numerous studies have examined the cost of macho displays in contexts ranging from aeronautics to manufacturing to high tech to the law. They show that men's attempts to prove their masculinity interfere with the training of recruits, compromise decision quality, marginalize women workers, lead to civil and human rights violations, and alienate men from their health, feelings, and relationships with others. The price of men striving to demonstrate their masculinity is high, and both individuals and organizations pay for it."

The key to this approach to safety is the emotional intelligence of the people on the projects; therefore the typical construction worker profile must be addressed first. We must start with emotional self-awareness so that workers are more aware of their surroundings, their bodies, and their levels of stress and fatigue. Then we should increase empathy skills, relationship skills, and social responsibility. That will make these types of programs successful. If we address these core issues, identify them, and take steps to improve them, we can create fundamental change that will help to take safety to a new level.

When people actually make emotional connections and care about each other, they look out for each other and work safer naturally. And when people work more safely, companies will save millions by lowering insurance rates, reducing worker's compensation claims, decreasing wrongful death lawsuits, and increasing productivity.

We have developed a safety program called Primal Safety®. This unique program states that everyone has the basic human right to go home alive and free from injuries at the end of the day. But with that right comes the responsibility to watch out for each other, to care for each other enough to point out unsafe situations, and to take the necessary corrective actions.

PRIMAL SAFETY®: A GUT LEVEL APPROACH

The costs for not working safely can be monumental both in financial and human terms. Most safety programs are comprised of objective rules and regulations. When it comes to safety, there is a right way and a wrong way to work. Even though there are severe consequences when these rules are broken, workers still may not follow these rules. Why is that?

According to philosopher, Ken Wilbur, these objective approaches such as rules, laws, and regulations, as effective as they are, will always hit a limit, a barrier. In order to break through this barrier, you must tap into the subjective side of safety, the primal side, the emotional side. Emotional responses are far more powerful than responses to rules and regulations. Once you tap into these emotional responses to safety, this objective barrier is breached and you will improve the effectiveness of your overall safety program.

Primal Safety° uses the following methodology:

Employees and project teams focus on emotional competencies such as emotional self-awareness, empathy, and interpersonal relationship skills. Key team members take the EQ-i® and develop the areas that are required for a successful program. Employees and project teams form closer relationships with each other with a deliberate approach to relationship building. Employees and project teams learn about each other's lives outside of work. This is done both formally and informally through activities for the workers and their families. Family members and loved ones become part of the safety process. Employees and project teams develop a greater awareness of safety – not because of rules but because the workers will care enough about each other to keep each other safe.

Primal Safety° program specifics:

1. The purpose of this program is to enhance the safety program that you already have in place.

2. The project team and any other appropriate parties take the Emotional Quotient Inventory (EQ-i®). This measures their emotional self-awareness, empathy, social responsibility, and interpersonal relationships. Without this foundation, typical construction EQ profiles will likely limit the effectiveness of this program. One of the highest competencies measured by the EQ-i® for construction folks is independence. Most of the folks in the industry defy death daily, working in a dangerous environment. It's like NASCAR drivers or bullfighters. There is an element of danger in what they do, and they are not fearful of death.

But with high levels of independence, most have the fear of being dependent on others. If you tell them to work safely or die, you may get a smile or shrug of a shoulder. But if you say to them, "If you don't work safely, your wife may be feeding you and wiping your bottom", they sit up and take notice.

3. The basic premise of the **Primal Safety®** program is that everyone in your company has a moral imperative to implement an effective safety program for all workers, including subcontractors, affording every worker the basic human right to go home each day uninjured to their family and loved ones. This means ZERO TOLERANCE! No accident or unsafe situation, no matter how small or insignificant, is acceptable. This approach is similar to how Bill Bratton, the former New York police commissioner, cleaned up the city. It was called the "broken window" theory. When there was a broken window, it was replaced. When graffiti showed up, it was removed the same day. There was zero tolerance of the smallest of infractions, because if minor infractions were not addressed, it led to larger infractions and more serious crimes.

4. All employees are encouraged to report any accident, potential accident, or unsafe situation, no matter how small. Every report is acted upon. Blame is not assessed, violators are not punished, and reporters are thanked and encouraged. The process is as follows:

a.   Analyze why the hazardous situation exists.

b.   Correct the situation.

c.   Educate the violators as to the proper means and methods in the spirit of learning and improving.

d.   Communicate these reports to everyone in order to avoid this situation in the future.

5. As part of the safety orientation, all employees watch a safety video. This video depicts interviews with workers who have been disabled by workplace injuries as well as interviews with their family and friends. The employees learn that these injuries not only rob them of their independence, but also create ripple effects that touch many people. There is a discussion after the video that reinforces this idea. This is a powerful way to make safety a personal issue.

6. All safety activities are tracked and recorded including accidents, avoided accidents, unsafe situations and behaviors, corrective actions, and communications. Everyone has access to this information, which is reinforced at all meetings.

7. There are numerous activities to reinforce these safety concepts.

Some ideas:

- At meetings, where possible, everyone should say their name and what they think about any safety issues for that day. They should be asked probing questions as well. According to the book, *The Checklist Manifesto*, the simple act of saying your name and giving your input makes it much more likely that you will speak up when something isn't right. When people don't verbalize their name and give their input, they are far less likely to say anything, even if they perceive that something is wrong. If this is not possible for large meetings, break your safety meetings down to smaller groups. And don't forget to have interpreters.

- The toolbox safety meetings should be fun and informative. You should not only discuss best safety practices, rules, and regulations, but address the emotional side of safety as well. We recommend walking safety meetings and mini-safety meetings. Walk around in large or small groups and point out safety issues like housekeeping, working from heights, scaffold and ladder safety, barriers and handrails, personal protective equipment, and any other safety topics that you find to be relevant. Ask them for their input. Ask them what they see. Ask them to point out what is wrong. We can provide more specifics on this to the project teams in charge of these meetings.

- Each morning, the entire project team does five to ten minutes of calisthenics and warm-up exercises. This reinforces the team approach to safety and prevents accidents by getting the blood flowing, warming up joints, and waking the team up mentally. We provide specific instructions to project team leaders on how to conduct this morning session. You may also use this session to highlight a safety issue for the day. According to a Swedish study on a construction project, morning warm-up exercises increased or maintained joint and muscle flexibility and muscle endurance for workers exposed to manual material handling and strenuous working positions. Over time, this will decrease the number of injuries and increase productivity.

- Safety milestones are celebrated with jobsite lunches and team activities. These celebrations are also an opportunity to enhance the spirit of the team and create closer relationships among the workers.

- There are social activities outside of work to encourage the workers to create closer relationships with each other. These may include sports activities, team sports, and other social activities.

- Celebrations of birthdays, anniversaries, births, life milestones, etc are encouraged. These celebrations reinforce the human side and put a face on safety.

- A focus on quitting smoking, good nutrition, weight loss, and exercise is a great way to let them know that you care about them as human beings. When they start implementing these concepts, their cognitive abilities will be increased. They will think more clearly, solve problems more readily, and work more safely.

- Any way to remind them is beneficial. Everyone could wear reminder bands or stickers. Or everyone could wear pedometers if you started a walking or biggest loser contest on site.

8. There are family/social activities that reinforce safety.

Some ideas:

- All of the children of the workers make safety posters encouraging their parents to come home safely to them each day. The posters are laminated and placed throughout the project. We have a **Primal Safety°** coloring book for all of the workers' children. The book starts out with a child's entire family going off to work on a construction site. Then it shows how his family stays safe all day long by tying off, using personal protective equipment, keeping the site clean, and working together. There are also a couple of "what's wrong with this picture" pages that will create dialogue about unsafe conditions. You can order these from my website (*www.brentdarnell.com*). All profits from these coloring books go to foundations that help families of those who have been injured or killed on projects.

- Put the photos of family members on hardhats along with their names. This will be a constant reminder of their loved ones and also create better relationships because everyone will be able to see your family and get to know them.

- There are family days so that family members can visit the workplace and see demonstrations of the safety equipment that keeps their loved ones safe.

- There are family social days such as picnics and parties. Every employee has someone who cares about his or her safety. Employees are not numbers. They are sons, daughters, fathers, mothers, brothers, and sisters. Find out which relationships matter the most for each employee.

- Workers are encouraged to take their safety equipment home and show their families how this equipment protects them from getting hurt on the job.

- Families are involved in the safety process. If there is a habitual violator, the family can be called in to help motivate that worker. This type of intervention has the potential to save lives.

- Many projects now have webcams for security and also to check in on the project from remote locations. What if you started a campaign where you gave the families the web address so that they could look in on their loved ones while they were working? You could post signs that say, "Work safely. Your family is watching you."

THE FUTURE OF SAFETY: Where do you go after you reach zero accidents?

For a moment, look to the future and see a vision where the construction industry is not only a safe industry, but actually becomes restorative. Imagine people working in this industry for years and retiring not only free from disabilities, but healthy and full of vigor. That is the next step in this process. Some say it is impossible to achieve. Some use the excuse that "this is a dangerous industry". Although there is no doubt that the work is tough and dangerous, we firmly believe that we can reach that level of health and safety through this emotionally intelligent approach and a true focus on people.

CHAPTER 4

STRESS, BURNOUT AND LIFE BALANCE ISSUES

The construction industry has always been stressful, but according to a recent global study compiled by the International Metal Worker's Federation, stress and burnout in the construction industry are on the rise around the world. Our workers are being asked to do more with less. The physical and mental demands are tremendous.

Many employees are working 60, 80, even 100-hour weeks, sometimes for extended periods of time. Take a look at some of the people who have been in the industry for a while. Many of them look older than they are and appear beaten down and worn out. Frequently, these workers develop stress-related illnesses such as heart disease (1 in 3 will die of this), high blood pressure, and diabetes, which is fast becoming a major epidemic. The CDC predicts that by 2050, nearly one in three will have diabetes.

A surprising number depend on nicotine and caffeine in the morning to get started and alcohol at night to calm down. Many use both prescription and over-the-counter medications to control the symptoms of stress such as headaches, stomach problems, allergies, pain, fatigue, decreased libido, difficulty sleeping, and irritability. I'm not sure about the statistics, but the improper work / life balance of most of the people in the industry certainly put a strain on relationships, and there are many divorces.

When managing projects, I used to visit the shiny white first aid box with the big blue cross on the door a couple of times a day. I would reach in and remove the small, individual packets of sweet relief, popping aspirin for my daily stress headaches. After wolfing down my lunch consisting of a chili dog and French fries from the roach coach (the endearing term for the break truck), I would reach for a few antacids as a preemptive strike on my afternoon stomach problems. It was much easier to pop pills rather than address the underlying stressors, which were the cause of many of these symptoms.

Many companies are beginning to wake up to this reality and address this issue. Using emotional intelligence, we can measure stress and burnout by measuring such traits as stress tolerance, self-actualization, happiness, and optimism. That way, we can determine if stress and burnout are problems and deal with them before they manifest themselves in the form of sickness, low productivity, absenteeism, and chronic disease.

According to Daniel Goleman, a leader in the emotional intelligence field, stress can be a killer, especially for those who have heart disease, the number one killer in this country. "Distressing feelings – sadness, frustration, anger, tension, intense anxiety – double the risk that someone with heart disease may experience a dangerous decrease in blood flow to the heart within hours of having these feelings. Such a decrease can trigger a heart attack." (5)

There is mounting evidence of this link between stress and general health. According to the World Health Organization, 80–90% of illnesses are either caused by or made worse by stress. They estimate that by 2020, the second leading cause of disabilities will be mental disease, including stress-related disorders.

In the United States, we give drug companies over $248 billion per year. Per capita spending on healthcare per year, which is $7,500 per person, is the highest in the world. (6) The use of antidepressants has doubled since 2000. Many of these drugs, both over the counter and prescription, are taken to alleviate the symptoms of stress and stress-related illnesses. Recent studies also indicate that there may be a link between stress and obesity, an emerging health issue in the United States.

Did you know that the United States is the only industrialized nation on earth without a paid leave law? It's no coincidence that we are also the most stressed nation on earth. In the United States, we simply don't have enough downtime. Compared to other countries, our holidays and vacation days are ridiculously low.

Most workers in other countries have a minimum of five weeks vacation and some have as many as nine. Even the Chinese have a law requiring employers to give their employees a minimum of three weeks of paid vacation. This may sound ludicrous to all of us hardworking, take-no-prisoners Americans. I've known several construction folks who wear their lack of vacation as a badge of honor. They boast, "I haven't had a vacation in ten years!" But what is the cost? We are becoming a nation of stressed-out people with autoimmune maladies, hypertension, diabetes, cancer, and heart disease.

We must change the way we think about our time off or face these dire health consequences. Europeans we interviewed said that they need at least three weeks of vacation because during the first and last weeks, they are thinking about work. With three or more weeks of vacation, they are able to have at least one week of total decompression. We just can't get there with a mere two weeks per year. We usually take those two weeks in installments of three and four-day weekends. It just isn't enough. With these diminished vacation times, we very rarely reach a true state of decompression, especially when we take our phones and check our emails each day. According to a study in the book, *Work to Live: The Guide for Getting a Life*, a yearly vacation was found to reduce the risk of heart attack by 30% in men and 50% in women. (7)

What if companies started offering more vacation time, more flextime, and more ways for their employees to recover? Even on projects, there are work processes that can be accomplished from anywhere. Could employees take a day per week or a day per month and accomplish these tasks from somewhere other than the jobsite? The costs would be minimal compared with the results. Most people we interviewed said they would take a substantial cut in pay to be able to have more time off. Just by investing a little bit into their people, companies would have happier, less stressed, more loyal, more productive employees.

Vacation is certainly one way to help deal with stress. But the day-to-day stress issues should be aggressively confronted by teaching managers to recognize symptoms of stress in their bodies, reduce these stressors, and build in recovery activities for renewal. This focus on stress reduction and recovery times allows them to have better performance mentally and physically. We teach managers how to handle their stress and create better life balance. One participant told us, "I have increased the balance in life, which has increased my efficiency at work."

One very effective way to renew the body is by doing yoga and meditation and practicing proper breathing and mindfulness techniques. Please visit my website and download the many resources that deal with stress. There is also a link to my book, *Stress Management, Time Management, and Life Balance for Tough Guys* and my guided meditation CD that takes you through progressive relaxation and visualization techniques. See Appendix A for details. By practicing these simple techniques, employees are able to reduce stress and create better focus. This work with yoga and meditation is outside the comfort zones of most construction folks. I remember the first day of a management development program for a large, international contractor. It was very early in the morning, and we were starting with basic yoga and meditation. The room was empty except for some yoga mats. There was meditative music playing. I watched as these tough construction guys entered, walked back out to make sure it was the right room, then slowly came back in and sat down on their mats.

The thing that surprises me most about introducing yoga and meditation to the construction industry is that almost half of the participants who have been exposed to yoga and meditation during our courses have continued these practices after the program has been completed. Even though some are reluctant to admit that they are actually doing yoga, they continue to practice it because of the tremendous benefits. Claus, a business unit president from Denmark said to me, "I think this yoga stuff is crap, but that deep breathing really helps me to reduce my stress."

Mariann, a controller from Sweden, was having trouble sleeping and sent me the following via email: "My job situation is extremely hectic again, and I have had some problems sleeping. Last night, however, I was able to calm down and relax using your meditation CD." Tom, a project manager from the United States put it this way, "Without question, the most helpful skill which I have implemented from my emotional intelligence training is how to better handle and reduce stress. By better controlling stress, I have seen positive results both at work and in my private life."

There is another benefit to yoga and meditation besides stress reduction. It actually enhances the emotional intelligence learning process. A recent study at the Indian Institute of Management in Bangalore found that yoga enhances emotional intelligence and improves managerial performance in organizations. Managers are better able to handle setbacks and they are less susceptible to stress. Because we are essentially rewiring the brain, creating new neural pathways, the yoga and meditation techniques help to create these new highways in the brain and speed up the behavioral shifts. We also use visualization techniques to improve emotional competencies. Participants will visualize situations and outcomes that reinforce the behaviors that they want to achieve. For all of you doubters, ask any good golfer what they do prior to making a shot. The brain doesn't know the difference between a visualization and the real thing. The process is exactly the same, and it creates learning and behavioral change.

Mindfulness is also a very powerful tool that we use. Jon Kabat Zinn teaches mindfulness techniques to executives. Mindfulness is simply being fully in the moment, not dwelling on the past or worrying about the future. Clinical studies have shown that these techniques reduce cortisol, the stress hormone, and increase DHEA, the youth hormone. It increases focus and makes you more efficient. And if you can't practice mindfulness all of the time, at least you can practice it during meals. Most of us wolf our food down or work during lunch. The average time to eat lunch for most kids is around 7-1/2 minutes. I encourage you to take at least 30 minutes for lunch and be fully present during your meal. Enjoy the tastes, enjoy how the food looks and smells and chew your food thoroughly. You not only enjoy your food more, you will likely eat less. It takes 20 minutes for your stomach to tell your brain that it is full. When you wolf down your food in ten minutes, your stomach still feels hungry and you have a tendency to overeat.

The more we study the brain, the more we see the connection between the mind and body. When we reduce stress, we reduce cortisol, a hormone that is secreted during the "fight or flight" response. Cortisol shuts down the thinking brain because when you are being chased by a lion, it is not in your best interest to over-analyze the situation. Without this hormone rush, we are able to think more clearly and solve problems more readily. We are able to be in a concept called "flow", where body and mind are in harmony with each other and both work as efficiently as possible. This results in fewer sick days and more stamina. Participants also report that they aren't exhausted at the end of the day.

Study after study confirms what we already know to be true. If we are sharp mentally, we function better physically and vice versa. Reducing stress through meditation has also been shown to increase the immune response and improve the body's healing process.

Yoga and meditation certainly aren't for everyone, but we encourage participants to find "their" yoga. For some it is a sport such as golf, hunting, fishing, sailing, or some kind of hobby or recreational pursuit. It may be music or exercise or spending time with their family. It may be taking a mindful lunch daily or going for a walk. Whatever your belief system and comfort level, you can apply these simple, but powerful techniques.

On one project we had laugh time. Every day from 3:00 to 3:15, we gathered in the trailer to laugh. Sometimes we told jokes. Sometimes we just laughed. It became this spontaneous thing that relieved tension and helped us to be more productive. This message of laughter has caught on in a big way. Laugh clubs are being formed all over the world. In fact, Glaxo and Volvo have organized laugh clubs in their organizations because of the positive benefits. No matter what you decide to do, the important thing is building in that reflection time and downtime each day where work is no longer the focus.

Companies are starting to realize the importance of addressing these health issues for their workers not only to make them more productive, but also to curb high healthcare costs. In an article titled, *"Wellness Program Cures Rising Health Care Costs"* (8), Cianbro Corporation, a large heavy civil and industrial contractor, addressed rising healthcare costs head-on. In 2001, they paid $11.5 million in healthcare costs, but these costs were projected to reach $20 million by 2004. So, in 2001, they started a voluntary wellness program for their employees. They reduced the percentage of smokers from 46% to 20%. 34% of their employees are exercising on a regular basis, and there has been a 20% reduction in hypertension and a 25% reduction in high cholesterol. Since 2001, instead of almost doubling, their healthcare costs have remained flat. They conservatively estimate that they get a $3.50 return per every dollar they invest in the wellness program, and this money goes straight to the bottom line.

The following participant came to us in total burnout. He was in a highly stressful work situation. He said he had no personal life. There was just enough time to go home, eat, and go to bed. He was overweight and smoking two packs of cigarettes per day. On his project, they were working a lot of long hours and there were a lot of unhappy people. His initial reaction to the program was negative. He didn't think the course would help him, and he had a difficult job to complete. Take a look at his before and after EQ-i®:

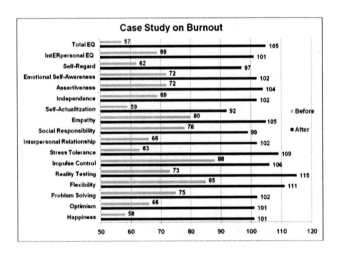

We initially focused on his emotional self-awareness. Then, we shifted to self-actualization and created a plan for the future. We also worked on stress tolerance and increasing happiness. The change in this participant was amazing. A change in five points is statistically significant and indicates a shift in behavior. Take a look at the changes. This is a new human being. In his words: "Without the program I would have never known where I was and how to get me out of the hole I was in. Look at these techniques and no matter how ridiculous you may think they are, just try them and see what happens to you. Because it does work." He lost 20 pounds, quit smoking, and was much happier with his life and work. The project was a big success and led to a promotion for this participant.

We have added a peak performance component to our programs using a symptom survey to assess which systems of the body are under duress. The amazing thing is that the results of this symptom survey correlate directly with the participant's EQ-i® results. One example: We worked with a fifty-year-old Senior Superintendent who had low impulse control and high assertiveness, which indicated a frustration/anger profile. He was a volatile person. He was overweight and couldn't lose weight even though he ran twenty-five miles per week. He told us he felt like he had no discipline and that he just couldn't lose the weight. But discipline was not his issue. His symptom survey showed that he had problems with sugar handling. His body was not effectively converting his food to fuel. He needed sugar like an alcoholic needs a drink, and he ate sugar all day long.

This caused his blood sugar to spike and then plummet, increasing his volatility. By working on the physical part (reducing sugar intake and dietary choices through a weekly food log) and the emotional part (increasing impulse control as it relates to eating and anger), this superintendent made great progress. His sugar handling improved dramatically along with his impulse control. He was no longer volatile. He felt better and had more energy. He created better eating habits, continued his exercise, and as of the writing of this book, has lost twenty-eight pounds. He is functioning at a higher level mentally, physically, and emotionally.

This high level of stress and burnout relates to other problem areas. Stress decreases productivity. Pete, a project manager sent me the following: "One example of the benefit [of stress management] for me is that I used to take painkillers regularly for frequent stress–related headaches. Now I have learned to deal with the root cause of the headaches, and I rarely take painkillers unless I am really ill." By addressing the underlying cause of these headaches, Pete is now less stressed and more productive. Burnout also contributes to high turnover rates. Employees may leave their jobs in order to reduce their stress. Stressed workers also tend to make more mistakes, which can negatively affect safety, increase costs, and reduce the bottom line.

CHAPTER 5

COACHING ALPHA MALES

It always begins with a phone call. A top manager will call me and say, "I've got this guy. He's a great guy, very competent and knowledgeable. But he's pissing everybody off. Can you help him?" I've had dozens of these calls about these alpha males. The industry is filled with them. They are strong, tough, highly motivated leaders who have a commanding presence and an aggressive style. These alpha males think they can do anything. My father, an alpha male in his younger days, tells the story of when he was a young carpenter. The layout engineer quit on a Friday afternoon and the superintendent asked my father if he could lay out the building. My father assured him that he could, then went home Friday to try and figure out how to lay out a building. He called a friend of his who brought over a transit and taught him how to use it over the weekend. In the end, he laid out the building without any difficulty.

These alpha males are extremely effective in certain areas, but according to an article titled *"Coaching the Alpha Male"* by Kate Ludeman and Eddie Erlandson, if these alpha males develop their interpersonal skills, they are even more effective. According to Ludeman and Erlanson, "Because [Alpha Males] believe that paying attention to feelings, even their own, detracts from getting the job done, they're surprisingly oblivious to the effect they have on others. They're judgmental of colleagues who can't control their emotions, yet often fail to notice how they vent their own anger and frustration. Or they dismiss their outbursts, arguing that the same rules shouldn't apply to the top dog." (9)

They further state "the best way to capture the alpha male's attention is with data-copious, credible, consistent data." Our goal is to provide undeniable proof that his behavior (to which he is much attached) doesn't work nearly as well as he thinks it does." We use the Bar-On EQ-i®, which gives the alpha male a graphical representation of his social functioning. If he is skeptical about the instrument, we can utilize the 360 EQ-i®, where the employees rate their own EQ while their subordinates, peers, supervisors, clients, family, and friends rate them as well. We do this to provide the "copious, credible, consistent data" that gets through to them. Once the alpha male sees this data, we have a better chance of convincing him that we can make him even more effective by improving his interpersonal skills. One participant put it this way, "Becoming aware of your own and other people's emotions makes you a powerful person."

If alpha males don't keep their assertiveness and self-regard in check, they can limit a company's financial success. As Daniel Goleman states, "A cranky and ruthless boss creates a toxic organization filled with negative underachievers who ignore opportunities; an inspirational, inclusive leader spawns acolytes for whom any challenge is surmountable. The final link in the chain is performance: profit or loss." (10)

There was an alpha male named Ragnar in one of the programs I facilitated. During one of the moments where we share our thoughts about the program in front of the group, he said, "When I first started this program, I thought all of you were stupid. But the longer I am around you, the smarter you become." Ragnar, who was extremely resistant at first, was saying in his alpha male way that he was becoming smarter and more in tune with his emotional side. At the end of the program he declared, "[The program] has, against all my own odds, made me human."

In the book, Joe Torre's *Ground Rules for Winners*, Joe Torre, the former manager for the New York Yankees, discusses how he dealt with the large egos in Major League Baseball. He says it's not about a command and control attitude, but about knowing and caring for these world-class athletes in a personal way. If they know that you care about them and are looking out for them, they perform well. In his words, "To develop this level of knowledge about your team players, you need some insight into their personal and emotional qualities." (11)

One of my favorite alpha male stories involves a superintendent in his mid-forties who was reluctant to accept the validity of this work. Although he scored high in assertiveness and self-regard and low on empathy and interpersonal relationships, he didn't see it as a problem. During our first session, he told me that he didn't really see a need to work on any of these competencies. He insisted that his job performance was excellent. And it was. I explained to him that I wasn't here to fix him because he wasn't broken. My job was to try and find ways to make him more effective.

I asked him to share his EQ-i° evaluation with people he trusted, and ask them if they thought he could benefit by embracing this work. They confirmed that he probably should work on his low scores. The more he thought about it, the more he was convinced that this would help his life and his career. So he made up his mind to give this emotional intelligence idea a try. Once he understood the concepts, he became highly committed to his personal development. He bought an Ipod and downloaded dozens of audio books. He applied the learning each day, and brought his entire project team in on the process of helping him to improve.

After about six months, during one of our follow-up discussions, I asked him if others had noticed any behavioral shifts in him. He asked his superiors to let me know if they had noticed any changes. His supervisor sent me the following email. I have changed the participant's name to maintain anonymity:

"Bill has worked with me since 1998, and the recent changes are nothing less than remarkable. Since starting with our company, his ability and potential were obvious, but Bill resisted the necessary behavioral changes required to realize his potential. In the past, Bill struggled to maintain working relationships with individuals that did not display his level of commitment and was not understanding of those with lesser abilities. This created a lot of friction over the years as Bill's work ethic, determination, and ability are not easily matched.

He is starting a new project (one of the largest retail projects in the company's history) as lead superintendent, and I think this will be Bill's opportunity to prove to all that he is truly one of our very best." Another superior added "I completely agree. Bill has really turned it around. I think he is a future star."

For the many alpha males in the construction industry, this emotional intelligence work can make them even more effective by tempering their dominant attitudes and behaviors with great interpersonal skills and impulse control. They will likely be resistant at first, as most construction managers and alpha males are, but once they see the benefits and become aware of the errors associated with their present leadership style, they doggedly pursue this work and become better leaders. They will also be able to more effectively deal with all of the project stakeholders and increase bottom line results.

CHAPTER 6

POOR INDUSTRY IMAGE

As most of you well know, the construction industry has a poor image. After performing my own informal survey asking many people about their experiences with contractors, their responses were invariably negative. Most contractors are viewed as unethical, untrustworthy, and difficult to deal with. I remember watching one of those Naked Gun movies. They lampooned just about everyone from law enforcement officials to politicians. When the villain was asked how he could do something so vicious, he replied, "It was easy my dear, don't forget I spent two years as a building contractor."

The *Jobs Rated Almanac* by Les Krantz ranks the top 250 jobs each year based on several factors of desirability such as pay, benefits, special perks, safety and security, stress risks, environmental conditions, physical demands, career outlook, and travel opportunities. One is the top rated job and number 250 is the least desirable. Year after year, construction industry jobs are rated at the very bottom. In 2008, there were a few construction related jobs that were ranked relatively highly: civil engineer (70), architectural draftsman (77), and architect (144). Construction foreman was ranked at 192. All other construction related jobs were ranked below 200. Of the bottom fifty jobs, sixteen were in the construction industry. (12)

Industry professionals have tried to address this image issue with little success. In the United States, The National Construction Image Steering Committee created the "Industry Image Initiative" to examine these image problems and explore potential solutions, but their progress has been slow. There was an editorial in the May 10, 2004 issue of Engineering News Record titled, "*Industry Image Initiative May Be Dying*". The editorial states that very little progress has been made to improve the industry image. In fact, it seems to be getting worse.

So why is our industry image so poor? I believe that it has to do with the attitudes of the people in the industry. From the age of fifteen, I worked every summer on various construction projects as a laborer, carpenter's helper, and layout engineer. I loved the work, but I didn't care for some of the people with whom I had to work. They were tough and aggressive. There was one foreman in particular who was downright scary to me. I was afraid to ask about anything for fear that I might appear stupid, and I never wanted to make a mistake. Think of the consequences of this attitude with regard to safety.

I remember a time when I stepped on a nail, but was so afraid to tell him, that I went home with a hole in my foot and a blood soaked sock. Back when I was working summers, the business was tough. Developing a thick skin was a must for survival. There was very little training or orientation. The attitude was, "Throw them in the deep end. If they can't figure it out, we don't want them here."

It was like some arcane fraternity, and the initiation process was difficult. These construction people with specialized knowledge would send me after non-existent "board stretchers" and "sky hooks". One time, my boss sent me to fetch a "come-a-long". Well, I had no idea what a "come-a-long" was, but I wasn't about to tell him that. I went to the tool shed and tried to find something that looked like a "come-a-long". Somewhere in the back of my mind, I thought that this was another wild goose chase similar to the "board stretcher" I tried to find the previous week. I was certain that when I returned, everyone would laugh at me. Despite these fears, I pressed on and chose something. By some miraculous twist of fate, I chose the right thing. Now, when I look back at these experiences, I think to myself, "What a screwy business, where you are so afraid of being the butt of a joke that you won't ask when you don't know something."

One other incident sticks in my mind concerning the attitude of the people in the business back then. I was an engineering student at the Georgia Institute of Technology and was working during the summer of 1979 as a layout engineer. We had purchased a Leibherr tower crane, and they sent a German engineer to help with the assembly and setup. We had poured a test weight with hooks embedded in the concrete for the crane to lift. The engineer asked me to determine the weight of the block. I pulled out my trusty handheld calculator along with my handy book that told me the weight per volume for concrete. I punched in the calculation and proudly wrote the result on the top of the concrete block.

Since I fancied myself to be an engineer, I wanted to be really accurate and precise so I carried the number out to six decimal places. When the engineer saw it, he called everyone around and said, "Hey everybody. Look here. Look what the college boy did. He figured up the weight of this piece of concrete." He took out a large Magik Marker, brushed off some of the stray aggregate and dust from the top of the block and marked through all of the numbers after the decimal. "Hey, stupid college boy, when you're dealing with thousands of pounds, you don't need so many decimal places. Or didn't they teach you that in school?" He then brushed more of the dust off, laughed, and said, "That dust I brushed off just changed your number." It wasn't a motivating experience.

Certainly this attitude has improved over the years, but there is still some work to do. It's no wonder that the numbers of young people coming into the industry are dwindling, especially in the trades. Because of these dwindling numbers, we have come to rely on immigrants to fill these positions. Without this influx of immigrants, we would not have the work force to build projects.

Several factors contribute to these dwindling numbers. Other industries usually have comparable pay and better benefits such as health insurance, paid vacations, sick days, and retirement programs. Other industries are not as dependent on weather and temperature as the construction industry. If there is a stretch of bad weather, some construction workers are simply not paid. The construction industry has made few adjustments to address these changes in the job market.

There is also a shift in demographics. Baby boomers are beginning to reach retirement age, and there are smaller numbers of generation X and generation Y to replace them. (13) And what about generation I (the internet generation)? All industries will be competing for this shrinking talent pool. Generation X and generation Y are motivated by a different set of values than the baby boomers. They want to be independent, but also feel like they are part of a family, part of a team. They want to be mentored, coached, and nurtured. They are also looking for more balance between work and family. And what will generation I bring to the workforce? We better start thinking about it now. We must develop the competencies to be able to deal with these future generations.

We have found two competencies that are consistently low for people in their 20s; reality testing and social responsibility. I believe several things cause the lower reality testing. These younger people live in virtual worlds of video games, emails, text messages, social networking, and chat rooms. When you ask a younger person if they followed up with someone, how many times do they say, "I emailed them." Future generations will say, "I texted them." My niece will sit with the family and text the entire time. Also, these younger generations see things in shades of gray. Boomers are more black and white in their thinking, which gives them higher scores in reality testing. The younger generations see all of the possibilities. They exhibit less right/wrong or black/white thinking. This can be frustrating for the boomers.

As far as the lower social responsibility goes, this is a little strange. Most of the cross-generational training courses that you attend tell you that these younger generations have high levels of social responsibility and that they want to make a difference in the world. And I believe that this is true from a philosophical standpoint. But the way the statements are presented on the EQ-i®, social responsibility is measured by individual involvement in socially responsible acts. I'll put it this way: If I told a group of people in their 20s that I was starting a litter pick up and recycling program, they would be very supportive and applaud my efforts. But if I asked them to give up their weekends to help pick up trash, most would likely be reluctant to participate.

I have heard the baby boomers' frustration with these younger generations, and some companies are finding it difficult to provide an atmosphere where these younger folks can thrive. We must be prepared to think and act differently to accommodate these younger generations and their values as best we can. Baby boomers are reluctant to do this. They believe that these younger generations are just lazy and don't have the same work ethic that they do. This is not entirely true. These kids are highly motivated and highly educated. They want to move up fast. They want to know what you know. If you throw these young folks into the deep end of the pool to sink or swim, if you ignore them and tell them to shut up and work hard, if you give them meaningless work so that they can pay their dues like you did, if you don't let them participate in important decision making processes, they will certainly leave.

These demographic and economic issues will be difficult to overcome, but there is one issue that contributes to this industry image problem that we can control. It is the attitudes of the people in the industry. What it boils down to is this human dimension. If we focus on leadership qualities like great interpersonal skills, we can greatly improve the industry image. These leaders must learn how to encourage workers and find what they are passionate about.

We must teach our leaders to communicate well, to listen and truly care about the people who work for them no matter what their age or gender. This will go a long way toward fixing this poor image while sending the message that this is an industry where you will be respected and encouraged to thrive. If we can find ways to improve this industry image, we will tap into this future workforce, improving clients' trust, working relations, and the way we do business. This will have a direct, positive effect on our bottom line.

CHAPTER 7

POOR CUSTOMER SERVICE

Ask most owners. The perceived level of customer service in the industry is quite low. Not long ago, the Vice President of a top five US contractor said to me, "I think the problem is that we just don't have enough empathy to understand and address the needs of our clients." Given the typical profile for most construction managers, this statement is undeniably true. As a group, most of these managers have low empathy skills, which can prevent them from providing great customer service. If this fundamental lack of empathy is addressed, along with other interpersonal relationship skills, customer service can be significantly improved. One program participant put it this way, "My interpersonal interactions with customers, colleagues, and subordinates have improved by being able to establish a deeper communication."

I had a participant, I'll call him John, a quality control person who was having some difficulty dealing with the representatives from the Corps of Engineers, who have a reputation for being very demanding clients. John scored very high in assertiveness and low in interpersonal relationships and impulse control. He told me that he really didn't like these Corps guys, and he tried to prove them wrong and punish them for their mistakes every chance he got. Most of the time, he just reacted to situations and relished the idea of making them look like fools. I asked him how that was working for him. He said that he felt like he was winning battles, but losing the war.

I had to find something that would work for John, something that would enable him to give the Corps better customer service. As it turns out, John was a devout Catholic. I asked him to picture the Corps representatives with "EGR" stamped on their foreheads. He asked me what "EGR" stood for. I told him, "Extra Grace Required". I pointed out that this was his chance to give them a gift they may not even deserve. He really liked this idea of applying his religious beliefs and implemented it with great results.

As he put it, "When faced with a conflict or difference of opinion, I've been very conscientious of letting others speak their minds while concentrating on their positions and feelings. This approach has produced positive outcomes, and I feel that by continuing to use this approach in difficult situations, I will improve and become more successful in resolving conflicts." His relationship with the Corps improved and enabled him to more easily close out the project.

I would like to share a personal example of poor customer service. I was having a very difficult time with a representative from a company who was creating my website. She was an extremely poor communicator. Sometimes, I thought that we were speaking two different languages. She didn't seem to listen or speak in a way that we both understood. She was very difficult to get along with and didn't understand my needs or try to fulfill them. In order to understand what my company did, she took the EQ-i®.

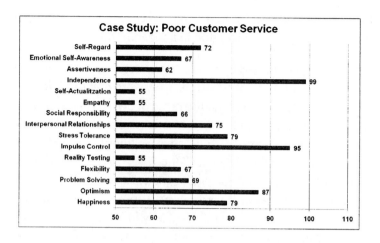

You can see from her profile why she was so poor at customer service. Her interpersonal skills were extremely low, coupled with relatively high independence, which means she probably would rather keep to herself than deal with anyone, especially someone with problems. She also had very low reality testing, which means she likely couldn't understand my situation or the nature of my problems. These traits, along with low flexibility and problem solving, were a recipe for customer service disaster.

Although I could not divulge this person's EQ profile, I talked to the president of this company about this employee's poor customer service. I asked him if he would be interested in a development program using emotional intelligence, coupled with learning modules on communication and customer service training. He declined the offer. I finally had to end the business relationship. How many customers is your company losing because of your employees' poor people skills?

It may not be enough to take your employees through "customer service" training. Given the typical construction managers' profiles, an eight-hour lecture stating a list of things to do to provide great customer service may not be effective since their lower empathy and interpersonal skills would prevent them from applying this information in a meaningful way.

I recently was engaged by a well-established top 200 contractor to deal with this type of situation. They were great builders, but when they hired a firm to get the pulse of owners in the area, the results were surprising to them. All owners admitted that they thought that this company built great buildings, communicated well, and were technically excellent. They also stated that this company wasn't as good with relationships, were difficult to work with at times and were not as fun to work with as their competitors. They now are strategically focusing on the human side of this equation and teaching their employees these emotional intelligence principles.

A couple of the top managers from this company awaited the return of one of their executives from a meeting with a potential client. When they asked him how it went, he replied, "We Brent Darnell'd 'em". In other words, he used all of the principles we talked about and applied them to this client meeting. He made it all about them and did not tout schedule, price, or quality. It went very well. They tell me that now BD doesn't stand for business development. It stands for Brent Darnell. They have found out two very important things:

1. Every company comes to the table with schedule, price, and quality. It is not really a competitive advantage. It is the price of entry.

2. When you compete on price alone, you become a commodity, but if you create a positive experience for that client and really pay attention to your customer service, they are much more likely to choose you, even if you are not the lowest bidder.

Companies must pay attention. Poor customer service due to a lack of people skills may be deteriorating client relationships while you are reading this book. If you address these fundamental emotional competencies now, you can improve your customer service. And improved customer relations mean satisfied clients, referrals, and repeat business, which has a direct impact on your bottom line.

CHAPTER 8

LACK OF TEAMWORK AND TRUST

D oes anyone else find it odd that the entire construction industry, to a large extent, is based on mistrust? One survey said that there were only two occupations with a lower level of trust than contractors: television evangelists and used car dealers.

We work in an industry where the owner doesn't trust the architect or the contractor, so the work is competitively bid and perhaps a construction manager is hired just to keep an eye on things. The contractor doesn't trust the subcontractors, so again everything is competitively bid. When you think about it, even the term "subcontractor" seems hierarchical and demeaning and doesn't suggest a sense of cooperation. The owner and architect don't trust the contractor, so they are constantly asking for verifications of pricing and methodologies. The contractor doesn't trust the architect or the owner, so he documents everything that is said and done to prepare for claims and litigation. When a problem is encountered, the process, from writing requests for information (RFIs) to processing a change order, is filled with negotiations, conflicts, and arguments.

One owner referred to RFIs as Requests for Income. The whole process is adversarial.

Imagine if everyone in the business increased their emotional intelligence, focusing on interpersonal skills, empathy, and social responsibility. When a project was begun, true teams would be created based on mutual trust. When a request for information was written, there would be enough trust so that the problem would be identified and corrected, and the contractor would be paid a fair price for the work without all of the back and forth arguments. They would, in turn, pay the subcontractors their fair share.

When I was a project manager, I suggested that we start calling our subcontractors "co-contractors", but my suggestion was met with blank stares or laughter. In Europe, they call these companies "entrepreneurs". Lee Evey, the former head of the Design Build Institute of America, suggests that we call them "specialty contractors". These names, as opposed to subcontractor, are much more conducive to creating a sense of team.

Think of the time and money spent on cover-your-ass documentation, disagreements, and negotiations on a project. If we could reduce this non-productive workload by creating true teams, imagine how teamwork and productivity would skyrocket. Everyone in the industry would benefit from such a shift, and everyone, including owners, architects, designers, contractors, and subcontractors would be able to add to their bottom line.

Take a look at the following project where lack of teamwork and trust slowed the job progress to the point where they called us for help. This was a $400 million tri-venture hospital project in California. The three contractors were at each other's throats. There was a total lack of trust, gossip was running rampant, and there were several personality conflicts. Teamwork was virtually non-existent.

Analyzing the situation using a systems thinking approach, we found what is known as a reinforcing loop. The lack of communication and information sharing caused team members to make assumptions, which were not always accurate. This misinformation led to a lack of trust, which caused the team members to be even more guarded with their communication and information sharing. This resulted in more mistrust, followed by even less information sharing and communication. The cycle continued to reinforce itself until they finally called us.

We call this reinforcing loop the "downward spiral to hell". I had a dream the night before this intervention where a fistfight broke out among all of the stakeholders. It looked like one of those bar room brawls in the movies. This was not comforting, but I pressed on. We first did an evaluation of the project team using the EQ-i®. That gave us some clues as to why they were behaving the way they were. Most had the typical construction manager's profile, which was exacerbating the conflicts.

We also performed interviews with the managers from the three companies. They were using words like "always" and "never" in their descriptions of situations and people on the project. This was an indication that they were definitely caught in this downward spiral. Using this information, we created a learning program targeting relationships, communication, vision, and team building. The first question I asked the group was, "What are the goals for this project?" There was total silence. Finally, after a minute or so, someone said, "Make money!" Okay, what else? They struggled to come up with an agreed upon list of goals. They were so caught up in the difficulties, they lost sight of what they were trying to accomplish. Then I asked them, "If you, the leaders of this project, don't know what the goals are, what do you think about those folks in the field?" It was a real eye opener. By focusing on the people issues and how their individual emotional profile may be holding the team back, we were able to re-establish the team atmosphere and increase their productivity and effectiveness. One of the project leaders,

Tracy MacDonald, a Project Director for McCarthy Construction, credited the intervention with saving the project.

Lack of teamwork can have even more dire consequences. For example, an editorial in the February 21, 2005 Engineering News Record titled *"Paris Accident Shows the Need for More Team Building"*, points out the need for cooperation in the industry. The lack of teamwork may have contributed to the partial collapse of a 640-meter long concourse at Paris Charles de Gaulle airport, which killed four people. The editorial states that, "The Paris collapse shows the need for all parties in the project delivery process to shake off the adversarial pressures and work more tightly as a team."

We must take a hard look at how we create teams. We've all been on projects with partnering agreements. You know the drill. Everyone agrees to work together and they all sign a big partnering agreement. Then they do a group hug and start the project. After a few weeks the problems start. People start peeing on bushes and establishing territories. The personality conflicts begin. The egos become entrenched. Everyone starts finding what they missed in the contract and develops strategies to overcome the deficits, usually to the detriment of other project stakeholders. It usually devolves into a mess.

There is a real push in the industry of more integrated project delivery systems with much more cooperation and teamwork. Integrated Project Delivery is a highly collaborative process, and there are rules of engagement and steps to the process. But we must make sure that we don't leave out the relationship part of that equation. We must take into account the typical emotional profile and how it relates to developing relationships.

If you engage in an Integrated Project Delivery process without addressing the fundamental emotional competencies of the participants, you will be setting yourself up for failure or diminished results. But if everyone took the EQ-i® evaluation and created development plans that included the context of working together on a project, if they knew their deficits and how they affect their interactions with each other, then the building process would be much more successful. This process also breaks down many barriers and brings people closer together. The lawyers will tell you that it is risky and that the contracts have not been worked out properly for this type of approach. But lawyers are all about shedding risk. This project delivery method is about sharing risk and creating great teams.

Paul Chinowsky and the University of Colorado, Boulder, is studying social network analysis or SNA as a way to improve team performance. By taking a hard look at group dynamics, trust, innovation, learning, and knowledge exchange, Chinowsky has developed methodologies to achieve high performance. Simply put, these social networks contribute to more successful projects by tapping into the emotional side of project stakeholders. This focus on the soft side yields hard results.

Perhaps all that project teams' need is a larger context. They tend to see thousands of small tasks and very rarely get to see the big picture. I drove up to a large renovation on an old Home Depot near my house. There was no signage out front, so I stopped by and asked several of the workers what business was going to be moving into the space. No one knew. How much engagement can there be when they don't even know what they are building?

I was doing a training session for McCarthy Construction, and we were trying to hone in on which elements contributed to good projects and which ones contributed to bad projects. One of the stories they told was very powerful. They had won the bid to build a cancer research facility for a hospital. Instead of the usual and totally ineffective teambuilding and partnering session, the hospital brought in a cancer researcher for the initial meeting. He told the project team and all of the stakeholders that one in three of them would develop cancer in their lifetime. This facility would be researching cures and preventive measures to reduce the number of deaths from cancer. He impressed upon them that they were building something that may some day save their life or the life of a loved one.

What a powerful, emotionally intelligent approach to the creation of a common purpose and a true sense of team! Even if you aren't building a cancer center, every structure has a purpose, whether that is creating homes for families, schools for learning, buildings for businesses to keep our economy moving, sports and entertainment venues for our pleasure, or infrastructure to help us create power, create fresh drinking water, remove our waste, or travel from place to place. I think we have all forgotten what a complex miracle construction is. Putting a building together is one of the most complicated processes you will ever encounter. On your next project, try tapping into that higher sense of purpose and accomplishment in order to create a true sense of team.

There are many software programs that share information and supposedly promote teamwork. But do they? Could technology actually hinder teamwork? We are constantly being bombarded with information, and everyone is tethered to their phones, constantly checking for emails and voicemails. I see it when I do program work. Now we make everyone surrender their phone to our cell phone jail for the entire day. Without this rule, the minute there was a break, everyone was on their device of choice, talking and texting.

The Georgia Tech football team did an interesting thing in their quest for the ACC championship in 2009. They took away everyone's mobile device. Before the phone ban, the coaches found that every time that the players had a spare minute, they were on the phone, texting and communicating with others. When the phones were taken away, they started interacting with each other more and became closer as a team. What if we banned phones in offices or on projects for short periods of time and encouraged more interaction among project stakeholders? Everyone would connect more, communicate more, and create better relationships and better teams.

These high performing teams are rare, but profound when they come together. Real teams need to have mutual accountability, but with the present project delivery methods that focus on shedding risk, this is impossible. Taking this concept to a higher level, what do you suppose makes a high performing team? One of the requirements is for every team member to care about the other team members and their personal goals, growth, and development. Again, we are tapping into that emotional side of teamwork, where the members create good relationships and have the empathy skills to understand the other team members' goals and aspirations. In short, they create great relationships with each other.

One of our participants put it this way, "I think relationships are very important in the construction business. Good relationships with clients mean repeat business, and good relationships with subcontractors mean successful projects." One of the books available through my website is Relationship Skills for Tough Guys. See Appendix A for more information. It teaches you how to establish and maintain relationships from the first handshake through the life of the relationship. We must pay attention to this emotionally intelligent, relationship-focused approach to teambuilding in order to create phenomenal, high performing teams whose successful projects will add more to the company's bottom line.

CHAPTER 9

QUALITY, PRODUCTIVITY, AND INNOVATION

How many times does work-in-place have to be removed because of other work that has been installed out of sequence? How many times does the communication break down and cause something to be delivered late or installed incorrectly? How many times do we improperly handle the architect's and the owner's expectations only to be ambushed during closeout and forced into reworking the finishes?

The Construction Industry Institute's research estimates that re-work costs on average 3% of total construction costs. This is money that is being robbed from your bottom line. During the Total Quality Management revolution and the six-sigma sojourns of the 80s and 90s, manufacturers vastly increased their productivity and decreased their defect rates. Unfortunately, the construction industry was virtually bypassed by that whole revolution. Productivity on most projects, even well managed projects, has been far lower than most manufacturers. In a recent productivity survey by FMI, a leading construction industry consultant, "53% of the respondents said that productivity had remained the same, decreased slightly or decreased substantially over the past five years." (14)

Low quality is also an issue on most projects because productivity and quality go hand in hand. One could argue that it is easier to control these factors in a manufacturing setting where there are repetitious work processes. This is undeniably true. But one can also argue that by exploring new, innovative methods, productivity and quality on construction projects can be dramatically increased.

There are many tools out there that are supposed to improve quality and productivity: building information modeling (BIM), web-based information sharing tools, computer-aided design systems, personal and handheld computers, digital cameras, lasers, automated transits, and project management and accounting software. And they do improve productivity to some extent. But how do we make that quantum leap to achieve the same high quality and productivity numbers as manufacturers?

And what about innovation? Innovation is a huge key for remaining competitive, yet most companies don't consciously promote innovation. How much does the industry invest in research and development? How many companies make a conscious effort to promote innovation? Why do you think that is? Take a look at the typical emotional profile for construction managers. Many have the control profile (low flexibility, high problem solving, and high reality testing) which causes them to be rigid in their approaches. This may serve them well in many ways such as adhering to plans and specifications, but with this rigid way of thinking, there is little innovation. New ideas are met with skepticism and rejection. We are all too gun-shy with risk. We can't try anything new. What if it doesn't work? A new product? An innovative approach to building? Let the other guy take the risk. This is also true for individuals. You learn quickly not to come to your boss with a new idea.

How many times do you hear the following?:

- We've always done it that way.
- We tried that, but it didn't work.
- Why try something new?
- Let's not take the risk.
- Just do it the way I told you to do it.

Most employees in the construction industry are linear thinkers who are not great innovators. So how do you cultivate a creative environment? By promoting innovation and creative thinking. We are all creative thinkers to varying degrees, but most technical folks would label themselves as not creative. This simply isn't true. Creativity is like a muscle. The more you work it, the better you are able to create. Companies should offer classes in creative thinking and innovation. From an emotional standpoint, individuals with high problem solving skills and reality testing along with low flexibility, tend to be very rigid in their approaches to things. But by working on flexibility and offering different ways of thinking about problem solving, we can improve the creativity and innovation of even the most rigid, linear thinkers.

Companies can also create environments that are more conducive to creativity. They can routinely do brainstorming sessions and panel discussions to explore new ways of doing business and innovative ways to approach projects. These groups should have a mix of young and old, newcomers and veterans. In these sessions, nothing should be censored, nothing should be too far-fetched. Once everyone starts participating in these processes, you will notice an increase in creative ideas, which will add to your competitive edge.

If you take a look at the typical EQ profile, you can see that if you improve the project stakeholders' emotional intelligence, especially in the areas of empathy, relationships, flexibility, and problem solving skills, we can improve quality, productivity, and innovation dramatically. Think about it. Many productivity problems on construction projects are caused by poor communication and poor relationships. Many quality control issues are due to poor communication and preparation and have little to do with expertise. High quality has more to do with motivating the workers to perform the work properly and managing the expectations of the owner and architect. Innovation is about creating environments where people feel safe to explore the possibilities. This is directly tied to the social competence of your project team.

Consider this apartment project where the mechanical, electrical, plumbing, and fire protection subcontractors had very poor working relationships. The project had a densely packed hallway, (is there any other kind?), in which the sprinkler contractor had to install his work prior to the ductwork, or his access would be cut off. The sprinkler contractor was behind and had not installed his piping. The duct man installed his ductwork anyway, knowing that the sprinkler man would have to pay him to take the duct down and reinstall it.

When the superintendent asked the duct man why he did it, he replied, "I got mine in per the schedule." The superintendent pressed him further. "Didn't you notice that the sprinkler man hadn't installed his work?" His reply was, "F#@! him! I've got a schedule to keep. If I had been late, you would have jumped all over my ass."

You can see several problems with this exchange. There was general lack of trust and communication among all of the stakeholders on the project, from the general contractor to the subcontractors. It caused much re-work, decreased quality and productivity, and ate into everyone's project fee.

Emotional intelligence can be used to improve productivity and the quality of the final product. It occurred on a housing project for the 1996 Olympic village in Atlanta, Georgia, which was being built for the state of Georgia (Georgia State Financing and Investment Commission or GSFIC). At that time, the GSFIC's contracts were difficult and their closeout procedures extremely demanding. Many of their projects took over a year after the certificate of occupancy to close out and receive final payment.

The project team had taken the time to do a lot of teambuilding and cultivated great relationships among the mechanical, electrical, plumbing, and fire protection subcontractors. We created shirts that put the name of all subcontractors on it along with the caption GOING FOR THE GOLD! This project had a similar situation, a packed hallway in which the sprinkler man needed to install his work prior to the duct. The schedule was accelerated due to some weather related delays, but the sprinkler contractor was not aware of this change.

The duct man had a great relationship with the foreman for the sprinkler company, and they often went out after work for a beer. Instead of installing his ductwork ahead of the sprinkler contractor, the duct man notified the sprinkler guy, and they worked out a way to install their work per the schedule, saving re-work and time. This great teamwork contributed to a highly successful project for all of these stakeholders.

In the end, the project was completed ahead of schedule despite seventeen straight days of rain during the foundation work and a damaging fire half way through the project. The key to the success of this project was relationships. Great relationships contributed to great productivity despite many setbacks.

Expectations of the GSFIC and the architect were managed so that everyone knew what to expect at the end of the project with regard to levels of quality. This resulted in a quick closeout. In fact, we closed the project out within 30 days, which was extremely rare for GSFIC projects.

Stephen Covey, author of The *7 Habits of Highly Effective People*, would call the focus on the crises a Quadrant I approach, or activities that are important and urgent. The focus on productive issues is a Quadrant II approach. These activities are important, but not urgent. If more time is spent in Quadrant II, less time will be spent in Quadrant I. This means higher productivity and more money to the bottom line.

Probably one of the biggest time wasters in the industry is meetings. Why do we have meetings? Think about the topics that are covered at most meetings. Do you focus on positive, productive issues such as teambuilding, vision, relationships, celebrations of milestones, celebrations of project goals, and other human aspects of the project? Or do you focus more on the crises and problems such as conflicts between contractors, owner and architect problems, non-performance issues, poor communication, relationship issues, and cover-your-ass posturing?

If the majority of your meetings are taken up with the latter, you may want to take a different approach. If you work to improve the people side of your project that promotes great relationships and positive communication, you will spend less time on the problems. Try taking a different approach to meetings. Always have a timed agenda, a time keeper and facilitator, but also make sure you put into the agenda some of the Quadrant II items. This will make meeting more productive and enjoyable.

Stress and burnout can negatively affect productivity. When we are tired and stressed, we aren't nearly as productive. When we work past our effective limits, productivity decreases. Some studies effectively argue that you can do more by working less. For many people in the construction industry, this is a hard concept to embrace. But according to one study, working past the point of fatigue increases problem-solving time by as much as 500%. How many times have you pushed yourself to complete a task only to have to do it all over again the next day? When you are tired, it is much better to take short, focused breaks in order to restore yourself and be more productive.

There was an article in the Harvard Business Review (June 2010) concerning Sony's efforts to make their employees more productive. What they found was that by taking more breaks and building in more recovery times throughout the day, their employees were much more engaged and productive. This was a hard sell to management, but the results are undeniable. Employees now take their lunches and build in uninterrupted time for important tasks and setting the course. They focus on four areas: physical health through nutrition, sleep, daytime renewal, and exercise; emotional well being and feeling valued and appreciated; mental clarity including the ability to focus and think creatively; and spiritual significance so that employees feel that what they are doing is important and goes beyond just profit.

I worked with one company who had a policy that their employees must keep their phones on twenty-four hours a day, seven days a week. I sat in a meeting with one of these employees who answered his phone five times during a one-hour meeting. This may seem like a good thing for customer service, but what is the cost to the employees? What kind of image does this project to other stakeholders? Ask yourself what percentage of phone calls are directly related to your customers' needs. Then ask yourself what percentage of phone calls are low priority time wasters and stress makers. Do you really need to be on call every waking moment?

Many companies are starting to pay attention to this lack of down time and stress-related issues and are offering a variety of solutions. Morning exercises stimulate the body and mind. Building in scheduled break times help employees to be more alert and focused when they return to work. Employees are encouraged to turn off their phones, and jobsite radios at these times so they are not constantly bombarded with work. Instead of working through lunches and scheduled breaks, employees are encouraged to have true downtime in order to recover and be more productive.

These group breaks also help with relationships and teambuilding, creating high-performing teams that naturally have higher productivity. By working well together they manage these relationship issues and minimize conflicts that interfere with productivity. They spend less time on non–productive activities and more time on activities that create meaningful results. In other words, they spend much of their time on Quadrant II activities, which are important, but not urgent.

Quality and productivity improve when we focus on people, and if productivity rises even by a few percentage points, margins increase dramatically. Take a look at the following example: You have a $25,000,000 project with $10,000,000 in labor costs and $1,000,000 profit. If you improve your productivity by 10%, your labor costs drop to $9,000,000. This would give you a profit of $2,000,000. In other words, with a 10% increase in productivity, you could double your profit!

CHAPTER 10

COMMUNICATION AND KNOWLEDGE SHARING

Knowledge is a firm's most valuable resource. More than 75% of the capitalization of the top companies in the United States is through knowledge and other intangible assets. (15) This is especially true in the construction industry where employee knowledge has great economic value. In fact, in most cases, it is our only competitive edge.

Lack of communication and knowledge management are closely related to poor productivity partly because they stifle innovation and problem solving. Until we tap into the emotional side of these issues, we will be unable to increase knowledge sharing and create true learning organizations. In our courses, we do a warm-up exercise called the Big Egg Drop. We divide into groups and see who can build the least expensive contraption that will catch a raw egg. After this exercise, I ask the question: "If we built this egg catcher again right now, could you build it cheaper, faster, better?"

Invariably they say "yes". But isn't this also true of our industry? Although each structure is different, the building components are fairly consistent. Do the knowledge and the lessons learned make their way to each new project? The usual answer is "not very often". Companies who have created lessons-learned databases find out shortly that their use is limited. Why is this? It is because people will only share information with someone they know and trust.

A large energy company learned this difficult lesson. They spent millions of dollars on knowledge sharing technology, but their employees were still not sharing their knowledge. They finally realized that technology was not the answer. Instead, they cultivated great relationships among their employees, which provided a web of knowledge that was available anytime. As As their CEO put it, "Since sharing knowledge is important only at the point and time when people need to solve a problem, the key to knowledge management is connecting people in a dialogue."

In fact, some technology may actually hinder productivity. I was talking to the president of a very successful project management software company about this issue. Although they have a great web-based software product that provides links for sharing information, some contractors still blame them for the lack of communication on a project. This software company is starting to realize that sharing information is not about the technology. It's about the relationships among the project stakeholders. Some companies have even created the position of knowledge broker to connect people within the company in order to share knowledge more effectively.

If we create these personal connections, if we establish true emotional threads, the employees will be more likely to seek advice and counsel from each other and create true learning organizations. If we cultivate the sharing of knowledge and innovative thinking, employees will contribute much more. This will ultimately contribute to increased innovation and productivity, higher margins, and a more robust bottom line.

CHAPTER 11

DIVERSITY, MULTI-CULTURAL ISSUES AND WORKING IN OTHER COUNTRIES

We have seen great changes in the cultural makeup of our work force in the past few decades. Many companies are expanding their geographic areas not only in the United States, but internationally. More women are entering the workforce. In short, we are encountering more and more diversity in this melting pot of construction. How does this affect the way we work? Are we prepared for these diverse cultures with their different values? Are we prepared to have more women in managerial roles? As companies are finding out, it's not just about learning another language or reading the book, *Men Are from Mars, Women Are from Venus*. Many different aspects of diversity affect the way we interact and do business.

The United States is made up of many cultures, and they all have different values and unique ways of working. Their sense of time and punctuality, their work ethic, and their own set of priorities concerning family, work, and personal time can vary a great deal. They will likely respond differently to situations in the workplace. If companies want to be more effective, they must recognize these cultural differences and try to make adjustments to accommodate them. It may be impossible to accommodate all situations in any given group, but we must make the effort to be aware of these differences and do the best we can.

There are also regional cultures in the United States. Doing business in the north is very different than doing business in the south. In the north, people tend to be more direct and assertive. In the south, this is seen as negative behavior. Southerners refer to these northerners as "Yankees". It is not an affectionate term. Companies in Florida and the west coast tend to have a much more casual workplace than companies in the northeast.

These cultural differences must be taken into account when doing business. These regional differences can be disastrous. One of my old bosses was a "Yankee" from the north and tended to be aggressive and blunt. We were presenting to a school board to build a school in South Georgia. We all drove down from Atlanta with our suits and ties and our well-rehearsed, slick, PowerPoint presentation.

When we arrived, the school board greeted us. Their dress was extremely casual. In fact, one of the board members, a farmer in the area, was dressed in overalls. Our "Yankee" lead presenter was blunt and abrasive and talked much too quickly. We came across like a bunch of "city -slickers" with our fancy computer presentation, trying to take advantage of these poor country folk. We would have been better off leaving the "Yankee" at home, dressing casually, establishing rapport with the board, and doing our presentation with posters.

For those companies working internationally, this cultural awareness is even more vital. Working in Europe, Russia, Latin America, and Southeast Asia involves a different set of rules. There are issues with bribery and corruption and other values. In China, "yes" doesn't necessarily mean "yes". It may only mean "I understand what you are saying". In addition, "saving face" is of prime importance. In Russia, you must be prepared to pay a "consultant" who will guide you through the intricacies of working there.

In the United States, we tend to be obsessed with time and punctuality. We like to dive right into meetings and try to reach a result in a short period of time. In Latin America, there is a more relaxed view of time. They also value intimate business relationships, which are cultivated over time. You would never discuss business during the first meeting there. These thoughtful approaches to the way culture affects business are crucial for successful projects and penetrating new markets.

I facilitated a program with a group of thirty construction managers from Argentina. We had a tight schedule, and I insisted that everyone come back from breaks "on time". The problem was that fifteen minutes past the time to resume, not one person had returned. I was trying to impose my US notion of "on time" on them. I finally got the message and adjusted the schedule based on their culture, because no matter what the consequence, they never came into the room at the scheduled time. I found out that in their culture, "on time" means up to thirty minutes past the agreed upon time.

We also created a different daily schedule. In their culture, they tend to start later and finish later. The 6:00 am yoga simply did not work for this group. We started around 9:00 am and did not eat dinner until around 9:00 pm. Making these adjustments when possible allows you to obtain the highest productivity from these different cultures. We must learn to ask ourselves, "Is it wrong or just different?"

The most multi-cultural program I've ever done was with a company called Nobia, a kitchen manufacturer, supplier, installer based in Sweden. This was a group of twenty-nine people from nine different countries. I was the only American. The first thing we talked about was cultural differences. Not only did we discuss country culture, but company culture as well.

Using a North American normative group, these cultural differences show up in the EQ-i®. The Argentines score very high in assertiveness, but very low in independence. It's a macho society, but also one with a high power distance. The boss is dictatorial and autocratic. The Chinese tend to score low in independence and assertiveness. The Europeans tend to score low in social responsibility because the governments take care of the disenfranchised. The Germans scored low in flexibility.

Once we had this discussion, we soon realized that there were some stereotypes that were based on real experiences, and some stereotypes that were not exactly true. We also realized that we were all human beings and had much more in common than we realized. All had some form of family. All had similar struggles. We capitalized on all of the things we had in common and shattered the stereotypes and minimized the differences that kept us apart.

One of the exercises for multi-cultural groups is called "the book title". I have a book for boys called *How to Be the Best at Everything*. I thought this summed up our American Culture very well. There is a touch of arrogance in that title and a real can-do attitude, which is so American. So, we divided into country groups and they had to come up with a book title that indicated their culture. The Swedes came up with *How to Be a Good Citizen and Not Stand Out*. The Germans came up with *How to Be Effective and Efficient*. The French and Spanish both came up with *How to Enjoy Life*. It's fun to see the different nation's take on society and culture.

Also, it was very interesting to see the participants as they used this discussion as a way to develop their emotional competencies such as empathy and self-awareness. This work brings diverse groups of people very close together in a relatively short period of time.

Some say business is business the world over, but smart companies are paying attention to the cultural dimensions of the places where they are working by making the necessary adjustments. Lack of understanding of other cultures can turn business triumphs into disasters.

Consider the story of the American entrepreneur who was getting ready to close the deal and sign the contract for a manufacturing facility in Russia. This American was a Mormon and didn't drink alcohol. In Russia, deals are customarily sealed with a vodka toast. The American served soft drinks. Because he did not embrace this honored custom of their culture, the Russians cancelled the deal.

Another cultural disaster took place when a Swedish construction company acquired a company in Poland. Poland, being a former Soviet country, had a very different culture. The bosses were stern and dictatorial. The boss told the workers what to do, and the workers did so without question. The Swedes, on the other hand, were very consensus-driven. They relied on the group to come up with the correct answers. This company sent some Swedish managers to Poland. Not knowing the culture, the Swedish managers had meetings with the Polish workers and asked for their input and ideas. The Polish workers assumed that the Swedes were inept. From their point of view, these foreign managers were so stupid; they were asking the workers to provide the answers! The Swedish managers lost the respect of the workers, and this initial setback took quite some time to overcome.

Where does this lack of understanding originate? Is it a matter of studying cultures, reading history and learning the language? Those efforts will certainly help, but these misunderstandings go beyond that. With the typical contractor's EQ profile, employees may have an even more difficult time because of their low empathy, low social responsibility, and low interpersonal relationships skills. To be able to navigate these differences, employees must develop these areas.

Jonas, a project manager from Sweden, put it this way, "When moving to a new job in a new country I needed to make people feel comfortable to tell me the truth. There were a lot of problems, which needed to be identified and solved. By using emotional intelligence, I think I got a good response, and I could, therefore, take quick action in creating a new structure."

Take a look at the demographics in the industry. There are certainly many minorities working in the field, but look at management. It's mostly white males. It is not very diverse. There are very few women in this male dominated industry, and the women who are in the industry are mostly in sales and office positions (56%). (16) Those in management positions (23%) have to walk a fine line between assertiveness and compliance. If a woman is too assertive, she is labeled a "bitch". If she is too compliant, she gets little respect.

We must learn to utilize the strengths of these talented women and embrace different approaches to project management. That will make our companies even more effective. In an article in Engineering News Record (November 15, 2010), they showed empirical data on women's role in business success. They cited studies by Catalyst LLC, a research firm. They found that "companies with more women board members significantly outperformed those with fewer female directors in return on equity, return on sales, and return on invested capital." Women will make up 50% of the overall future workforce, and all industries will be competing for them. It would be wise to think about how companies can entice women to enter the construction industry.

Many companies are combating this diversity issue with diversity training. But if companies don't address these underlying emotional issues (low self-awareness, social responsibility, and empathy), diversity training can be a waste of time and money. These attitudes toward women and minorities are not very conducive to a diverse workforce. And if these attitudes don't change, we will lose these capable women and minorities to other industries. We could be driving away the future. An article in the October 30, 2000 Engineering News Record predicted that the construction industry would need to attract more women and minorities in order to grow. This prediction has come to pass and is even truer today.

Once these emotional skills are improved, it is much easier for employees to see other points of view and establish and maintain good relationships, despite the differences. And unfortunately, empathy and interpersonal relationship skills are always the two lowest scores. This is vital for doing business in these diverse workplaces so that we can create more of a team atmosphere and make our workforces more productive. This higher productivity will lead to a less stressful working environment and a better bottom line.

CHAPTER 12

SUSTAINABILITY AND ENVIRONMENTAL ISSUES

According to the United States Green Building Council, the demand for "green" buildings is rising dramatically in the United States and around the world. This increase is fueled by the advantages that green buildings have over conventional construction. The buildings are more energy efficient, conserve water and resources, have lower long-term maintenance costs, and generally last longer than conventional buildings. There is also less exposure to an increasing number of lawsuits related to toxic mold and Sick Building Syndrome.

There are advantages to the occupants as well. Studies show that they are more productive and have less sick days. They experience better indoor air quality, more natural lighting, and more comfortable work environments. In a California study, a school was converted to a day-lit school with the addition of skylights. After the conversion, the students performed 5 to 14% better on reading, language, and math skills as measured by the California Achievement Test. (17) In a hospital study, surgery patients in rooms with natural lighting needed less pain medication. (18)

This green building trend also has advantages to contractors. By reducing, re-using, and recycling materials, contractors can save a bundle of money on their waste removal costs. As anyone in the construction industry can tell you, these costs are increasing due to limited landfill space and higher tipping fees. I was the Environmental Manager for Skanska USA's Atlanta office when we implemented an environmental management system in order to be certified in ISO 14001, an international environmental standard.

During the first year, Skanska's Atlanta office saved over $270,000 in waste removal costs and diverted thousands of cubic yards of waste from landfills. During the implementation of this system, we encountered some resistance, especially from the guys in the field. They complained that they didn't have time, couldn't train everyone, and didn't have room for recycling dumpsters – the list was endless. What was the source of this resistance? I was at a loss until I began learning about the power of emotional intelligence.

Take a look again at the typical construction EQ profile (Chapter 1) and the relatively low scores in social responsibility and empathy. Low scores in these areas indicate that these workers may have difficulty seeing the global picture, the effect of their actions on others, and the interconnectedness of everyone on the planet, which is essential for embracing these environmental concepts.

This green building trend also relates to teamwork. The United States Green Building Council's LEED® (Leadership in Energy and Environmental Design) program is a certification process for green buildings. It takes a high performing team involving all project stakeholders to deliver such a project and receive the certification. Without this sense of team, these green projects are quite difficult to complete.

I worked on a LEED project where the relationships were difficult. The owner hired a construction manager who pitted the architect and designers against the contractor. If the project did not achieve LEED certification, both the architect and the contractor would have to pay $50,000 in liquidated damages. The owner thought that this was the best way to limit his liability, but in fact, it made the LEED process quite difficult. The process became more about blaming each other and shedding risk instead of working together as a team.

Environmental issues can impact a company's image as well. Skanska, a multi-national Swedish contractor, learned this hard lesson at the Halland Ridge Tunnel project in Hallandsås, Sweden. A subcontractor was using a grout containing acrylamide, which contaminated the local groundwater. In the United States, this may have resulted in a small article in the newspaper, but in Sweden, there was a media frenzy surrounding this story. As a result, Skanska's reputation was badly tarnished. They have since overcome this environmental debacle with a stronger focus on environmental issues. The entire company now has an environmental management system, and each business unit is certified in ISO 14001. This focus on environmental issues has improved their image and led to more business opportunities worldwide.

The green building trend is here to stay, and the demand for green buildings will only increase. If you are entering into this market, you will do well to address these emotional intelligence competencies prior to any technical training. This will give your people the tools they need to be able to understand and implement these green building strategies, improve your company's image, and capture more of this emerging market. This will, in turn, create opportunities for business and eventually increase the bottom line.

CHAPTER 13

HUMAN RESOURCE PROCESSES

HUMAN RESOURCE PROCESSES such as hiring, review processes, turnover, training, retention, and succession planning:

Hiring and Recruiting: New research has determined that a bad hire can cost as much as two to three times their annual salary. Yet most companies continue to make the same hiring mistakes. For someone who makes an annual salary of $80,000, the costs for making a poor hire can run upward to $240,000! Most companies to whom we have talked have insufficient processes in place for recruiting and hiring. These processes consist mainly of impromptu interviews. Few, if any of the managers have been trained in interviewing techniques. The lack of effective hiring processes can be costly.

A leader at a top five contractor here in the United States confided to me that they end up hiring "the best of the worst". Of course, this was true when the economy was booming. To prepare for the future and a better economy, companies can make better decisions by determining what skills are required for each position and whether or not the candidate possesses those skills. A great way to match these skills is by using the EQ-i® evaluation. Before, it was difficult to measure soft skills such as empathy and interpersonal relationship skills during the interview process. Now we can measure these traits and make better hiring decisions.

Recently, we received a call from an extended stay hotel company who was interviewing for a mid level management position. After an initial interview, they had some concern about the candidate's interpersonal skills, and there were indications that this person may be a micromanager. So they decided to invest in an EQ-i® evaluation. The evaluation showed that the candidate had good interpersonal skills, but showed relatively low flexibility and low self-regard along with high problem solving skills and reality testing, which could manifest itself in the form of micromanaging.

We recommended some behavioral type interview questions to make sure that these areas would not be a problem. To address the flexibility and potential control issues, the company asked, "We value letting our employees stretch themselves in their positions. Can you tell us about a time in your work history where you had to be very flexible and let subordinates do things their own way?" According to the company's managers, using the EQ profile was a great way to avoid hiring the wrong person. And companies who avoid making bad hires will save money.

At the writing of this book, we are starting to pull out of the worst economic downturn since the Great Depression. When things ramp up, and they will, most companies will be scrambling for talent again. They will crisis hire without any processes in place and create problems for themselves down the road. Prepare in the lean times to be able to hire the right people and make sure you have a process in place. In addition, if you work on your employees' emotional intelligence and focus on teaching them how to create great relationships, you will be better prepared. The internal relationships will improve your entire business, the external relationships will create new business, and the ongoing relationships will generate future business. In addition, the connections that your employees have will help you to find the best people when you begin to ramp up your hiring.

Review Processes and Retention: Can you remember when people worked for the same company for their entire careers? This is no longer true. It is estimated that generation Y will have 10 to 14 jobs by age 38. A recent article in Engineering News Record discussed the high cost of turnover. Catherine Santee, Senior Vice President of Finance for CH2M Hill stated, "All of us are fighting for talent." Michael Creed, CEO of McKim and Creed added, "We've finally realized we're in the people business." (19)

So what makes people stay with companies for longer periods of time? Of course, there are issues such as compensation and benefits, but if you want to retain great employees, you must look beyond those numbers. In short, if employees feel valued and taken care of, if they are offered ways to develop themselves, their job skills, and their life skills, they will stay with the company longer. This is especially true for younger generations. Health and wellness is also becoming more and more important to employees. If you can offer ways to keep your employees healthy by offering classes and a comprehensive wellness program, they will be more likely to stay.

According to a 2003 Mercer Survey, half of the companies surveyed reported that their employees receive little or no ongoing performance management training and very little ongoing feedback and communication. Most contractors do not have meaningful review processes that discuss career goals, personal goals, and developmental needs, while some companies have no review process in place at all. Without these reviews, employees tend to feel unappreciated and disengaged.

According to the Gallup Organization, most people leave companies because of poor treatment from their immediate supervisor. Many times, this poor treatment manifests itself in a lack of appreciation. If companies improve the EQ of their supervisors and teach them to create a meaningful dialogue with their employees, the employees will feel valued and appreciated, and their level of engagement will increase. According to the ISR, a research and consulting firm, high engagement companies improved their operating incomes by 19.2 percent while low engagement companies declined 32.7 percent during the study period.

Managers can engage employees by discussing their developmental needs and helping them to improve. Managers can also use the information for succession planning by determining what competencies are required for future positions, then helping the employee to measure and improve them. If employees know there is a plan for their future, they will naturally be more engaged and are more likely to stay put. Some employers use training and development programs to honor and reward their star employees.

If we ignore our employees, if we let them stagnate, if we don't offer them a plan for their careers, we will be faced with ever-rising turnover rates and unproductive, unmotivated, disengaged employees. But if we use emotional intelligence to develop managers and employees, to make them more valuable, and to address personal and professional development issues, they will feel appreciated. They will value the company who provides this type of development and will be much less likely to look elsewhere for employment.

Some companies are using the latest technology and social networking sites to promote this sense of connection and feedback, especially with the younger generations. Employees now can tweet (send a short message) and ask for specific feedback. Or managers can tweet the employees to let them know how they are doing and how they can improve. This can be done daily if necessary. This constant feedback along with praise for doing a good job is essential for keeping employees engaged. It also makes them feel valued. For the younger generations, this is how they communicate.

Succession Planning: One of our clients, an engineering firm, has a succession plan that ensures continuity. The two people directly under the CEO are in line for the CEO's position. These positions are thoughtfully filled with the next leaders of the company. When these two heirs apparent took the EQ-i®, we identified some areas that they could work on in order to be able to eventually step into the CEO role some day. This organization realized that the skills these individuals utilize now are not the same skills that they will need to run the company. This kind of evaluation and purposeful development for key positions is essential for good succession planning and successful leadership.

Another big issue in the construction industry is stalled career paths. It happens time and time again. When a technically trained or educated person is adept at managing processes, they are promoted. They keep getting promoted until they are no longer managing processes, but managing people. And that is when things tend to go awry. They believe themselves to be intelligent and may have highly developed technical knowledge and expertise. Some even have postgraduate degrees in their fields. So why can't they manage people? This frustration often leads to burnout or even worse, demotion or termination. I've seen it enough times to say that it is a trend, indicating a definite need to teach these potential leaders the "soft skills" needed to break through these career barriers.

Another issue associated with succession planning is filling those middle management positions. Most companies have talented young people and seasoned veterans, but there is a dearth of good, qualified, middle managers. The thing that is usually missing from these young managers is the maturity and the people skills needed to step into leadership positions. By focusing on their emotional intelligence, we can teach them people skills and transition them into leadership positions in a shorter period of time.

Recently, the CEO for a top 50 contractor asked, "What if these guys don't improve their interpersonal skills? Do we fire them?" The short answer is that we must try to match the skills to the position. Although we have not found this to be true, if an employee continues to have low scores in interpersonal skills, despite efforts in training and development, you may be able to find a position where these skills are less important, where they don't have as much interaction with key stakeholders. Putting people in the right place to make them more comfortable and productive is essential for increasing overall productivity and the bottom line.

Training and Development: Is your company wasting money on training and development? Training, for most companies, is about as effective as rearranging the deck chairs on the Titanic. Daniel Goleman refers to corporate training programs as the "Billion Dollar Mistake". (20) Actually, in the United States, the cost could be much higher than that. According to the American Society for Training and Development, in 2007, corporations in the United States spend $129 billion on training. You would think that spending money on training would be a good thing. But is it?

Most training is event based and informational. Participants come to a training event and are given loads of information, usually in the form of a lecture or PowerPoint presentation. Normally, there is very little follow-up or coaching. The facilitators of these events tell you the following: If you can just take one nugget from today, the class will be worth it. I think this is a copout. I call these training events "three-ring binder" programs. I'm sure you've attended programs where you listen to an eight-hour lecture and take your three-ring binder home, only to forget what you learned and go back to your normal routine in a few days. You put your three-ring binder on a shelf, and a year later, when you need the binder, you take out the contents and throw them away. I think this approach to training may be a sales scheme thought up by binder manufacturers to sell more binders.

There is one other training phenomenon I have seen repeated over and over. And companies waste millions of dollars each year. They will find a book. I call it the "book of the year". Some examples of the book of the year are *Good to Great, Who Moved My Cheese?, The One Minute Manager,* or *The Fifth Discipline.* Don't get me wrong. These are all great books. The company will hire a keynote speaker for their annual manager's meeting, and they will listen to a session on the concepts from the book. They will find their hedgehog or talk about finding new cheese or how to be a better manager. There is no application, no follow-up, no learning, and no behavioral change. In a few weeks, it's back to business as usual, and when the planning committee plans their next company meeting, they decide that the previous book didn't create any changes, so they try to find the next book. The problem is not in the book. The problem is in the application. These companies fall into that old training trap. They think that information and awareness creates behavioral change. It doesn't.

These approaches to training are ineffective to say the least. The Vice President of a Federal bank recently told me of an internal group that had horrible communication, personality conflicts, and rampant gossip. They lacked the ability to function well as a team. When I asked about her assessment of the situation, she told me that they were sending them to a ropes course. Now I have nothing against ropes courses. They can be quite entertaining and may ease the superficial issues of such a group for a short period of time. But the underlying issues are never addressed, much less resolved. The emotional competencies that are contributing to the turmoil are not discussed, and there is no fundamental change. The group members tend to revert back to their old ways within a few short days.

If you take a group of construction folks with the typical construction manager's emotional intelligence profile, and try to teach them some type of interpersonal skill, they may not have the emotional makeup or the right tools to be able to implement what you are trying to teach them. The wiser strategy is to start with an evaluation of their emotional intelligence. This will not only provide a foundation from which to work, but it will allow you to target specific areas for development. You will have laid the proper foundation to ensure that all future training will be applied in a meaningful way.

We use the latest neuroscience to develop program content and delivery so that participants will actually apply the information and create behavioral change. We use hands on, experiential learning, role plays, and discussions in our classroom. We get up and move and do a lot of reflective learning and self-directed learning. In addition, it is vital to include coaching and follow-up. Without accountability, it is human nature to set these development strategies aside. We use the principles in a great book called *Brain Rules* by John Medina. According to this neuroscientist, the following brain rules apply:

- Our brains evolved while moving. You have to get people moving in order for them to learn.

- Emotions more readily create memories that you can recall. We tell lots of stories to reinforce the learning. Jesus taught in parables for a reason. It is easy to remember the lessons.

- Repetition-repeat to learn, learn to repeat. We do many reflective learning exercises throughout our programs and there is continuous follow-up and coaching. We encourage participants to roll this learning into their review processes and meet with accountability partners on a regular basis.

- Sleep is vital to preparing your brain to learn and retain. We encourage proper sleep and nutrition to prepare your brain for learning.

- Stress will prevent you from being able to learn. We teach participants how to relax. We also have the cell phone jail. Participants must turn in their cell phones for the day. They can't get them out of the jail until the end of the session. If you're worried about an email or a voicemail, it is impossible for you to absorb information from the session.

- Use all senses. Although vision is the most developed sense, all senses should be used whenever possible. Participants listen to music and have in depth discussions. They perform hands-on, kinesthetic exercises. They practice mindful eating and drinking. They watch videos and look at other visual media. There are stories about students studying for tests while smelling peppermint. When they sniffed the peppermint during the exam, they recalled much more of the information compared to a control group

- Curiosity creates a sense of wonder. People will want to learn if you challenge them and increase their curiosity.

Companies can now stop throwing money away on training that is soon forgotten. By using this EQ methodology to evaluate, measure, and improve these emotional competencies, and by utilizing ongoing coaching and follow-up, companies can create fundamental change from within instead of imparting information that will never be applied. Visit my website (*www. brentdarnell.com*) for case studies and documentation that supports this training methodology to create true behavioral change. And if you want to take a look at peak mental and physical performance, we have combined the emotional intelligence work with peak performance in our Total Leadership Program. See chapter sixteen for more information or visit *www. totalleadershipprogram.com.*

CHAPTER 14

Frequently Asked Questions

Isn't this just another one of those personality profiles?

Invariably, several program participants tell us they've already taken all of these kinds of tests and that this is nothing new. Many of them have taken the Myers-Briggs or the DISC test. There are literally thousands of these tests on the market today. Most are based on preferences – you know the types of questions – would you rather read a book or sail a boat? For people with low self-awareness, this can be very informative and fun, but most of these tests are rather limited for detailed, personal development.

For those who are somewhat self-aware, these tests are merely confirmations of what they already know. In fact, the common response is, "Yep, that's me. So what?" It is my belief that personality tests, without some kind of context, are limited in their application to personal development. When you take a personality test, you put yourself in some general state of mind. But the choices that you make on those tests may change based on the circumstances. I may be more of an introvert in my personal life, but at work, I'm an extrovert. So how do I answer those questions? Sometimes I would rather be the center of attention, and sometimes, I would rather be alone. They very rarely capture the true nature of the person. These tests simply can't capture the complexity of a human being.

This approach to development using personality types is very prevalent in the training industry. Participants take a test to find out their "type". Usually there are three other "types". You are either a color or a number or a quadrant or an animal. Then, they teach you about the other three "types" and how to get along with them. This approach is limited at best and can be dangerous. First of all, human beings are far more complex than a single "type". Second, unless you carry the tests around for everyone to take, it takes empathy to determine what the other person's "type" is. And empathy is not our best emotional competence. In fact, for most groups, it is the lowest score. Third, for some people, this is a real copout. They will stereotype people into whatever "type" they determine and treat them a certain way, which may or may not be correct.

Once you develop your emotional skills, you will be able to deal with any type of person in any situation. You will have the self-awareness to know how you are feeling and how you are being perceived and the empathy skills to know how they are feeling. These situations are dynamic. They can come up in an instant. Isn't it better to have good fundamental emotional competence to work from rather than rely on a set of "rules" for certain "types"?

A construction company I worked for used the DISC profile for all of its employees. DISC is a test that indicates the following personality archetypes:

- Dominant tends to be direct and guarded
- Interactive tends to be direct and open
- Steady tends to be indirect and open
- Compliance tends to be indirect and guarded

As it turned out, 80% of the people in our construction company were "Dominants". What does that tell you? Most people in the construction business have a dominant style. They tend to be direct and guarded. Didn't we know that already?

Myers-Briggs, another personality test, indicates the following traits:

- Extraversion versus Introversion E or I
- Sensing versus iNtuition S or N
- Thinking versus Feeling T or F
- Judging versus Perceiving J or P

When you take the test, you are given a Myers-Briggs Personality Type. But what are you supposed to do with that information? There are some Myers-Briggs modules on teambuilding and how to deal with other Myers-Briggs types, but how do you know the personality type of everyone you encounter? One company made everyone put their Myers-Briggs profile on their coffee cups, but this concept was a miserable failure.

Let's take a look at another case study, a thirty-year-old financial consultant who could not keep a job. She was a top of her class MBA from an Ivy League school and her IQ was 138. Most of the time, she was hired on the spot. But she went through six jobs in four years. One of her clients actually brought a lawsuit against her.

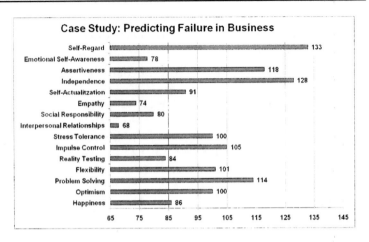

Case Study: Predicting Failure in Business

We can see from this case study that "a very high independence score and a very low interpersonal relationship score suggests that she is a loner, perhaps due to a serious inability to relate to others. Moreover, her difficulty in empathizing with others contributes to this inability to relate to people and to feel part of the larger social context."

When this woman took the Myers-Briggs, she was an ESFJ (Extraverted Feeling with Introverted Sensing). But the results of the Myers-Briggs gave her little information about why she could not hold a job. After taking the EQ-i®, she could target specific areas for development that helped in her pursuit of a career.

With personality tests, your results rarely change throughout your life, and if they do, it probably has more to do with the context in which you took it. You may shift slightly as you age. The other problem is that there is no clear path to development. If you are an ESFJ, do you want to become an INFT? And how do you do that exactly? What are the development strategies to get you there? There are none. Simply knowing yourself better does not create behavioral change that you need to be able to attain your goals. We say it over and over in our courses: Awareness alone will not change behavior!

The EQ-i® is a very different tool. It measures specific competencies such as empathy, assertiveness, and problem solving skills. It is very dynamic and reflects what is going on in your life and work at the time. If you are going through a difficult time, it will be reflected in the scores. This is much more valuable information. And when you look at that snapshot and where you want to be in the future, it becomes extremely practical. Then you choose areas to develop, and a detailed development plan is created utilizing specific development strategies. There is practical application, measurement, and improvement. This creates fundamental behavioral shifts. Personality tests simply do not do that.

Is there a correlation between emotional intelligence and performance?

I facilitated a program for a top 100 contractor based in the southern United States using emotional intelligence as a foundation for leadership development. After the managers were evaluated, I ranked their interpersonal scores (empathy, social responsibility, and interpersonal relationship skills) from the highest to the lowest. This company had their own ranking system in order to identify their star performers, the ones who contributed most to the success of the company. The astonishing fact was that the company's overall ranking and the ranking of interpersonal skills correlated almost one-to-one. This told us that the managers who had the best interpersonal skills were also the company's stars. They were the managers involved in the most profitable projects who contributed the most to the company's bottom line.

Multi-Health Systems has a program called *Star Performer* where companies look at the EQ-i® profiles of their star performers for particular departments or positions and determine with statistical accuracy which emotional competencies are essential for high performance. Then it is just a matter of recruiting, hiring, and training for those competencies. The drawback to this approach is in the performance criteria, which must be objective. For sales, performance is objective and clear. For project managers, it is less clear. You may have a high performer that loses $100,000 on a project that would have lost $1 million. Or you may have a low performer that makes $500,000 on a project that was supposed to make $1 million.

Can emotional intelligence be learned?

Seabiscuit was just a broken down horse incapable of winning until someone saw his potential and developed it through training. It was only then that he became one of the greatest racehorses in the history of racing. The trick is to be able to identify individual potential and develop it with effective techniques. But how do you teach something like empathy? We have developed a methodology targeted for the construction industry called "Emotional Intelligence – Foundation for Your Future". It was co-developed with Kate Cannon, a pioneer in the field of emotional intelligence.

After the initial EQ evaluation and feedback, we begin with a half-day program where each participant creates detailed, individual development plans. The participant targets specific competencies based on their future needs and then chooses development strategies from different categories depending on their learning style. They also create plans for mental and physical peak performance that are tied into their emotional plans focusing on nutrition, exercise, and stress management. We utilize many different types of exercises and development ideas and use various media such as books, fables, movies, television, magazines, operas, plays, and websites.

We also emphasize the day-to-day application of this learning and provide inspirational quotes for each competency. In addition, we build in many levels of accountability. In a group setting, everyone has an accountability partner. They also provide me with accountability partners above them, beside them, below them, family and friends, and clients. After the six-month mark, I call these accountability folks to see if they have seen any changes.

These are all powerful ways to keep the learning in the forefront, but the key to this learning is in the follow-up and coaching. We contact individuals every three or four weeks to check on their progress, offer encouragement, and provide coaching. We also do at least one face-to-face coaching session during the program. Without this individual coaching and follow-up, the participants tend to set aside their development plans. But if they know they will be re-evaluated and that someone will be checking in with them every few weeks, they are much more likely to work on their development plans and create fundamental behavioral change from within. One participant said this about the process, "I thought that people are who they are by their mid-twenties. I definitely feel that people are capable of significant change."

The following is a graph of a leadership program I did for a top 200 contractor:

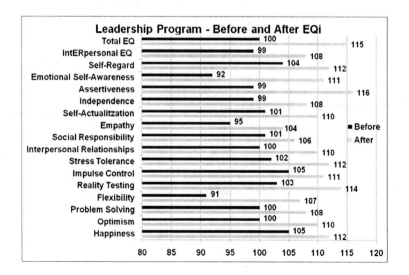

Note the significant changes. Keep in mind that a change of five points can indicate a shift in behavior. Many of these changes are in the double digits. Before the program, ten competencies out of seventeen were at or below the mean (100). After the program, there were no competencies at or below the mean and eleven out of seventeen competencies were at or above the above average range (>110).

We have an empathy exercise that is extremely effective. Keep in mind that most of our participants are men. We instruct each participant to go home from work, dismiss the children, turn off the television, sit their wife down and ask her to tell him about her day. He cannot solve any of her problems, offer any suggestions, or make any comments during her monologue. The only thing he is supposed to do is try to understand the feelings she experienced throughout the day. The only comment he can offer is "that must have made you feel …"

After the wives overcome the initial shock of this, they are quite pleased. In fact, several participants reported a spark of romance after this session. Talk about positive reinforcement for developing your empathy skills! Once the participants can tap into the power of empathy, they are motivated to apply it in the workplace. By truly listening and putting themselves in the shoes of subcontractors, owners, architects, and other project stakeholders, they find that they are much more effective in their day-to-day dealings with them.

I love to tell the story of Bryan, a superintendent in his late thirties with an anger problem. He told me that this problem had troubled him since he was young, and that if I could help him find a way to control it, he would be most grateful. This issue showed up in his EQ-i®. He had low emotional self-awareness along with high assertiveness and low impulse control. His low emotional self-awareness didn't allow him to feel himself getting angry, and eventually, with his low impulse control, it just boiled over.

The first thing we did was work on his emotional self-awareness. I suggested that he try to become aware of where he felt anger in his body and identify it as early as possible. We also worked on basic breathing and meditation techniques along with centering techniques to help with his impulse control.

I gave him a book to read and told him that it may be a little "out there" for him, but to try and find something he could relate to. In the process of reading the book, he found a centering technique that worked for him. He created a focal point by putting a photograph of his two small girls on his mobile phone. When he felt himself getting frustrated, (with greater emotional self-awareness, he felt it in his body), he excused himself from the situation, took ten deep breaths, flipped open his phone, and looked at his little girls. This allowed him to decompress and control his anger.

In his words, "Leaving a bad situation, even briefly, has allowed me to not act in anger or impulsively." He improved his emotional management and changed his behavior, making him a more effective leader. With this shift, he has learned to listen more without being so reactive. He told me that the people who work with him have noticed these changes. As he puts it, "Listening, not reacting to people I encounter has led to a more positive approach to my professional life." In addition to improved leadership skills, there has also been an improvement in his mental and physical performance. He is less stressed and better able to handle difficult situations without compromising his health.

Even if the scores from the EQ-i® do not increase; there still can be some very useful information for the participant. Annelise, a purchasing manager from Denmark, decided to work on her social responsibility, which was relatively low. Eleven months later, at the end of the program, when she took the EQ-i® again, she found that her social responsibility score was even lower. Interestingly enough, her self-actualization, happiness, and optimism had increased dramatically.

When we discussed these numbers, I asked her why she chose to work on social responsibility. She told me that she believed that it was the right thing to do, that she thought her family and friends wanted her to spend more time with them. I asked her if she had spent more time with family and friends in an effort to increase her social responsibility. She replied that she had not. She told me that work had been particularly hectic, and she had been working non-stop since the beginning of the program. She usually worked alone rather than in groups or teams. She also indicated that she felt a little guilty for working so much.

I asked her if she enjoyed working and she responded by saying that it was the most important thing in her life. She loved the challenge and felt that the company needed her during this particularly difficult period, which made her feel valued and important. That was the reason for her significant increases in self-actualization, happiness, and optimism. I suggested that perhaps this second evaluation revealed that during this period in her life, her work, which gave her great joy, was something that she would do well to focus on. In addition, since she worked alone, this way of working did not contribute to increasing her social responsibility. This conversation was a great relief to her. Perhaps all she needed was permission to enjoy her work life without guilt. So, in this case, although the competency she had originally chosen decreased, the results of the second EQ-i® gave us some real insights into the direction she wanted for her personal and professional life.

Isn't this just another management fad?

I have given much thought and introspection to this question. As a matter of fact, I considered this possibility when I first started this work. But after seeing the results and seeing the supporting data, the answer to this question is a resounding NO! The shelves are filled with thousands of self-help books for managers. And many of these books contain good information. So, why do management fads come and go like the tides?

Because there is a fundamental flaw in their application. They pile generic information on top of generic problems without regard to the individual. No matter how good the information is or how valid the approach, without addressing the fundamental emotional makeup of the individual, the application of this information may never take place.

Every company we have worked with agrees that communication is essential in the construction industry. Companies spend millions of dollars on training to give their people better communication skills. But because of the typical EQ profiles of most people in the construction industry, they are often incapable of applying this training. If they have high assertiveness, independence, and self-regard, and low empathy and interpersonal relationship skills, they will likely come across as someone who doesn't listen, won't ask for other's opinions, and does whatever they think is best regardless of any group input. You can put that person in a communication seminar or buy them books to teach them how to communicate, but it is very probable that they will still be unable to communicate effectively when the seminar is over.

If someone has high reality testing and problem solving along with low flexibility and optimism, they may have issues concerning change. This person will have a very rigid approach to life and work. This person can go to a seminar on change management or read a book like *Who Moved My Cheese?*, but his lack of flexibility usually prevents him from truly embracing change. He will have difficulty in the construction industry because of the constant change, but if his flexibility and optimism are increased, he will be much better able to deal with this issue.

Using emotional intelligence as the foundation for development programs is a different approach. Instead of starting with a particular area of training such as communication or teambuilding, we address the fundamental emotional developmental needs of every individual. Then we address these needs with specific, targeted learning modules. By addressing the emotional competencies first, the participants can develop the emotional makeup to be able to apply the concepts of the learning modules. All future training can be related back to the employees' emotional intelligence development plans, which also make any subsequent company training more effective.

As Lisa Fanto, the Senior Vice President for Hardin Construction put it, "I've been in and managed corporate education for a long time, and I've seen all of the fads du jour come and go and suffered through many of them. This is the only thing I've seen ever in my career that actually changes lives. I know that sounds dramatic, but it does. It actually changes people. And in order to change the way people manage, you have to change the way they live."

CHAPTER 15

How Do We Get There From Here?

A Step-by-Step Methodology for Improving Emotional Intelligence

"Things do not change; we change".

Henry David Thoreau

We have learned many lessons from these programs over the years. We have learned what works and what does not work. We have developed a very good methodology that is highly successful. Here is the step-by-step process.

1. Learn more about emotional intelligence. There are many books on the subject. Discuss the basics and the options.

2. Choose a consultant. Be sure that you choose someone who is certified to administer evaluations and give feedback. It is also important that the consultant understand your business and the way emotional intelligence relates to improving it.

3. Choose an evaluation tool. The Bar-On EQ-i® is an excellent self-assessment tool, but there are several very good tools

on the market. MSCEIT® is another instrument that measures EQ. The difference is that MSCEIT® is an ability based EQ evaluation instead of a self-assessment. You may choose to do a 360 evaluation where the employee measures his own EQ, and subordinates, peers, bosses, clients, family, and friends evaluate him as well.

4. Start with the top management. Then move on to a group of managers in your company whom you believe will benefit from this type of work. The selection   process should be well thought out, and the participants should be given a quick overview of emotional intelligence prior to taking the EQ-i®.

5. Have participants take the evaluation and receive individual feedback. Make it clear that these evaluations are confidential and will not be shared with anyone in the company. We emphasize that the EQ-i® is a snapshot in time, and ask each participant to think about what they need going forward personally and professionally.

6. Have each participant create detailed development plans. We take several different approaches here. Some companies choose to work on the emotional competencies and leadership. Others bring in the physical and mental peak performance component. Participants can develop integrated plans (peak performance and EI) or individual plans based on their needs and the needs of the company. This preliminary work will give participants a better understanding of themselves, their limitations, and what to work on. We have developed a module called Emotional Intelligence – Foundation for Your Future, which discusses what emotional intelligence is, why it is important, and how to develop it. Even if we don't incorporate peak performance, we always give the participants the option of a general development plan. While we are in this process, it's a good time to focus on areas in your life you want to

change-finances, health, a new hobby, quitting smoking, eating better, etc.

We also do some initial exercises to set a baseline. One is called the Four Quadrants. Participants divide a piece of flip chart paper into four quadrants and label them family, work, personal, and hopes/dreams/aspirations. At the top, they put their name and their favorite piece of music. At the bottom, they put some of their challenges both personally and professionally. This is a great exercise. It breaks down barriers and creates a lot of emotional threads among the participants. We keep this information for each individual forever so we can check in occasionally to see what has changed.

We also have them write a letter to themselves dated the last day of the program that lists all of their accomplishments that they have attained as a result of the program. This future diary plants all of their accomplishments in their subconscious so that even if they aren't thinking about them consciously, they are still working on them. Recently, we have given the participants the option of making a mind movie, which is a visual future diary. There is a website that can facilitate this process, and you can even post your movie on You Tube. This work at the subconscious level is very powerful. We use relaxation, visualization, and self-hypnotism to change those old tapes in your head so that you can achieve all that you want to achieve. This focus on the subconscious level facilitates the creation of new neural pathways in the emotional part of your brain. In fact, in a recent study at a management institute in India, they found that people who regularly practiced yoga and meditation had higher levels of emotional intelligence.

7. Determine the group scores and address any group developmental needs. For the construction industry, these needs usually lie in the area of interpersonal skills

and emotional self-awareness. Reinforce this emotional intelligence learning process with learning modules such as communication skills, relationships skills, teambuilding, negotiation skills, coaching, and motivation. Teach the group about stress management and time management. These learning modules may also include areas specific to the company or group such as business strategies and vision. The programs we provide are truly customized to each individual, to each group, and to each company. And with minimal lecture and self-directed, experiential learning, each program is truly unique.

8. Spread out the learning process. This type of emotional learning takes place in a different part of the brain than cognitive learning. It's not like solving a problem. It is more like learning a language or learning to play a musical instrument. It takes repetition and internalization over a longer period of time. We recommend a minimum of nine months to one year. In our experience, after the initial excitement of starting a program wears off, there is always a lull. After continuous follow-up and coaching, this lull is overcome and progress is made. We generally start to see behavioral shifts at the four to five month mark. After nine months, this behavioral shift is fairly permanent. Then, we give the program a few extra months just to be sure that the transformation is permanent.

9. Create an atmosphere of learning, not an atmosphere of training. We also use the latest studies in neuroscience that tells us how people learn and retain information. Mobile phones are turned in for the day. They are not even allowed to check them during breaks because if they are worried about an inflammatory email or voicemail, they will be dwelling on that instead of participating in the learning process. We involve as many of the senses as possible during the learning process. We utilize reflective learning continually because repetition creates retention. We get

people out of their seats as much as possible because we learn better when our bodies are moving.

10. Build in accountability. Without it, there is less focus on learning and less behavioral change. Build in as much accountability as you can. Ask participants to roll this work into their review process. Ask them to involve as many people in their journey as possible. We require a list of accountability folks who are above them, beside them, below them, a family or friend, and a client or someone outside of their company. After six months, we call every one of these accountability partners and ask them if they are seeing any changes in the participant.

11. Coach the participants during the learning process. This ongoing coaching will reinforce the learning and hold the participants accountable for implementing their development plans. Without coaching and follow-up, there is little change. See the following graph. I worked with a group of higher level executives for one day to show them the process that their direct reports were experiencing. They took the EQ-i®, received feedback, and created detailed development plans. They had the best intentions of carrying those plans out. Then I went away. There was no coaching or follow-up.

Fast forward three years. Because the most common comments we get from participants is, "My boss needs to take this course," these same guys ended up in a full blown course with coaching and follow-up. They re-took the EQ-i®. Look at the scores between the first and second EQ-i®. Basically, nothing changed. The only two statistically significant changes (5 points or more) were flexibility, which went up by five and interpersonal relationships, which went down by five. After the year-long course, take a look at the results on the third EQ-i®. There were statistically significant increases in many areas. Their behaviors had definitely changed.

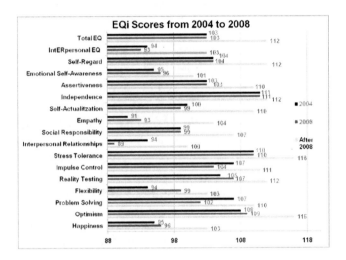

EQi Scores from 2004 to 2008

12. Have the participants retake the EQ-i® evaluation and receive individual feedback. Discuss the changes in the scores and what they mean as well as the individual's EQ development plan and behavioral changes.

13. Provide a wrap-up session where participants discuss their before and after scores and what they mean in terms of their development. Celebrate the accomplishments and analyze the shortfalls, then end with a discussion of how to create lifelong learning. Re-evaluate the development plans and modify accordingly. We check in with our four quadrants to see what has changed. They read the letters that they wrote to themselves. We watch the mind movie. Then, we take all of this into account, reflect on it, ask ourselves where we want to go from here, then create development plans going forward filled with accountability.

14. Have the participants check in annually to see where they are in their development. Their professional and personal situations may have changed, and they may need to focus on different areas. They should be re-evaluated and receive

individual feedback as a part of the follow-up procedure. Take a look at the following graph:

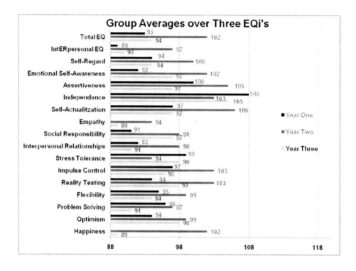

The initial EQ-i® was prior to the Total Leadership Program in September of 2008. This was followed by plan creation and a year of coaching and follow-up. The second year was at the end of the Total Leadership Program, which was September of 2009. Participants took the EQ-i® again. You can see that significant progress was made. Remember, a change of five points or more can indicate a shift in behavior. Then the participants created new plans for the following year (2010), but there was no coaching and follow-up and no accountability. The third EQ-i® was taken for the reunion (September 2010). You can see that in most areas, they are right back where they started from in 2008.

Without the coaching and follow-up and accountability, the participants reverted back to old behaviors, which are re-flected in the EQ-i® results. It is vital that participants check in annually and that companies create ways to hold them accountable. Otherwise, the return on investment in training can be diminished.

15. At this point, the participants may need more coaching and reinforced learning modules to address new areas of learning.

16. For individuals, you can start on your journey to improve your emotional intelligence today. The first step is to take the EQ-i® and receive feedback. The next step is to work through our workbook and create a development plan. Contact us to set all of this up for you and send you the workbook. If you want to see how the process works, you can take our mini EI test, which is available in our download center. There is also a free, edited workbook which will enable you to create a plan going forward. We don't recommend the mini EI test for detailed personal development, but it may help you to target some areas that are problematic.

We have many online resources that will help with this ongoing development. Visit our download center at *www. brentdarnell.com* and take a look in Appendix A.

LESSONS LEARNED: There are several errors that companies have made with regard to this emotional intelligence work. In order to avoid these mistakes, be aware of the following:

1. It is a good idea to take top managers through this type of evaluation and training first. Make sure this work is aligned with the company vision and values. We had one participant who told his boss he was working on empathy. His boss replied, "No you're not." His boss thought that empathy equated to weakness and this company was not going to show weakness. You don't want participants to return to their jobs to find resistance to these emotional intelligence concepts. If they are working to improve their interpersonal

skills while senior managers are neglecting theirs, they will be frustrated. Senior management must know what this work is and support it fully.

I talked to one company that I thought would be a good fit for this type of work. They had a daycare center in their offices. When I gave my pitch to the HR manager, he told me that he didn't think the company would embrace this emotional intelligence work. I asked him about the daycare center, and he told me that the only reason they had a daycare center was because it encouraged the employees to work longer hours. With this type of company value (work extremely hard until you have a heart attack and die) emotional intelligence simply won't work.

2. Build in as much accountability as possible. You can't have too much. For each class, there are accountability partners in the class. We also ask for accountability partners above them, beside them, below them, a client, and a family/friend. We tell them that we are going to call these folks after six months to see if they are noticing any changes. Make sure they know that you will be following up with them and their accountability folks throughout the program.

3. Be sure to include follow-up and coaching in the program. When there is no follow-up, participants treat the program as another one of those training programs that wastes their time and yields little practical results. When you work with each individual to create a development plan, coach them through it, and follow-up with a second evaluation and interview, it encourages accountability and gives the program credibility. And when the participants know there will be follow-up, they are much more likely to work on their plans and create fundamental behavioral change from within.

4. Don't be discouraged if all of the participants don't embrace this work. It takes some time to win the skeptical

construction folks over, but in the end, nearly all embrace this work and create that fundamental change. There will be some who will never value emotional intelligence work. In our experience, this is less than 5% of the participants. But even those who don't participate fully seem to get something out of the program and find at least one thing that helps them in their life and career.

5. Make sure that the style of teaching is effective for the group. We use a maximum of 20% lecture and PowerPoint. The other 80% is experiential learning, self-directed learning, group discussions, role-plays, and hands-on exercises that relate to the latest neuroscience studies on learning and retention. We take great pains to understand the company's business objectives and make sure the learning is practical and applicable.

6. Many training companies are repackaging their canned training programs and referring to them as programs on "emotional intelligence." Let the buyer beware. Make sure your consultants are qualified. Check their credentials and their certifications. Ask for references and focus on past results. Make sure that their evaluation instruments are validated. One of my colleagues refers to these un-validated tests as "Ladies Home Journal" tests. Although they can be entertaining, they should not be used for personal development.

CHAPTER 16

The Total Leadership Program

We have taken this mind/body connection to the next level. We have created a program called the Total Leadership Program where we combine mental and physical peak performance with emotional intelligence. We saw tangible correlations between the physical evaluation and the emotional evaluation. And when we focused on both, our results took a quantum leap.

This program grew organically. We always give the participants the option of working on something besides emotional intelligence. Keep in mind, many of the groups I work with are middle-aged men. Over 90% of them chose health. They wanted to lose weight, quit smoking, eat better, exercise more, and reduce their stress.

We have created a customized peak performance program for these construction folks. That way, we can get a baseline and see if the program has had a positive effect on their level of performance both from a physical and mental standpoint.

We are seeing patterns in typical physical profiles and how they match the EQ-i® profiles. For instance, whenever we see low impulse control and high assertiveness (frustration, impatience, and anger), we now ask the person if they have a poor diet and eat a lot of carbohydrates and sugar. And many of them have said yes. One of the participants told us he never realized how much diet and exercise affected his emotional state and problem solving capability. Another participant told us that since she has cut out sugar during her day, her problem solving capacity has increased tremendously. She told us that toward the end of the program, she received an out of sequence bonus, a raise, and a promotion. She also improved her mental and physical performance dramatically.

A very large, multi-national contractor sent two people to our last Total Leadership Program. They told them that they were sending them to this program to make some changes or be fired. I told the HR person that we don't fix people, but we would certainly do our best. At the end of the program, both participants not only survived a round of over 300 layoffs in their west coast offices, but one was promoted. In addition, they both changed their lives for the better. They had better relationships with family members, were better able to cope with stress, and were generally much happier. The HR person who sent these people told us, "You saved two very valuable employees. And you can bet that if they are still working with us, they are "A" players."

Another company, a medium sized glass installation company, brought ten participants because they saw the value of the program from the very beginning. Many of these participants were high school educated, blue-collar workers, and they made huge changes in their lives and work.

This program changes people's lives and transforms companies. If you want more information, visit the website at *www.totalleadershipprogram.com*.

Chapter 17

Final Thoughts

My wife and I were in Amsterdam and took in a concert at a very famous concert hall called the Consertgebouw. We heard Nigel Kennedy, a brilliant violinist, but quite different from any violinist we had seen before. He wore his hair in a spiky Mohawk. He wore boots and a silk coat unlike the members in the orchestra, who all had white ties and tails. The first thing he did was take down the velvet ropes that separated the audience from the orchestra. With a great flourish, he said, "Now we are united!"

During the concert, he acted more like a rock and roll star than a classical violinist. He rocked back and forth with orchestra members and danced around the stage. At one point, he walked off stage while playing and came back on kicking a soccer ball. Continuing to play, he kicked the ball out into the audience. It was a delight watching his passion and his great musical ability.

At the end of the concert, I leaned over to my wife and said, "I want to be that guy. I want to be that weird guy who is passionate about what he does and gets great results even though people look at him as someone who is a little bit out there." She thought a minute and said, "You teach emotional intelligence, yoga, and meditation to contractors. I think you are that guy."

I love this industry and am proud to be an engineer. I remember as a kid going to the jobsite on Saturdays with my Dad. This was before OSHA of course. I and my three brothers would ride up in the buck hoist and run wild on the floors of the high rise inching our way toward the edge of the building where the only thing that stood between us and certain death was a couple of thin steel cables. It was exhilarating. I was in awe that my dad could be a part of this. And every time we drove past anything that dad worked on, we always said, "That's Dad's building" or "Dad built that building." There was always a sense of great pride.

I understand the reluctance of the people in the construction industry to embrace this work because it is outside of their comfort zones. I probably won't grow a Mohawk, but I will continue this work with passion and enthusiasm because I have seen emotional intelligence change people's lives and transform companies.

We have been grappling with these construction industry problems for decades, perhaps centuries. Isn't it time we focused on the root causes of these problems and addressed them head on? When I saw the connection between the typical emotional intelligence profiles and the major industry problems, I felt like Marlon Brando's character, Walter Kurtz, in the movie *Apocalypse Now*. I had this sudden insight "like a diamond in the middle of my forehead."

If companies begin to realize that people are their most precious resource, if they are willing to take a chance and use this incredible tool called emotional intelligence, they will begin to hire the right people, nurture them, promote their personal development, give them direction for their careers, plan for succession, decrease turnover rates, and increase retention. In addition, this will facilitate increased customer service, teamwork, and productivity. In turn, accidents, stress, and burnout will decrease. Their employees will be healthier, happier, and more productive.

Companies that embrace this work will improve the industry image so that young people will flock to our ranks, and our sons and daughters will carry on this proud tradition of contracting. What's the alternative? If we let things continue as they are, the industry may be in trouble. Our inaction could cripple construction, but our focus on people will lead us to lasting solutions.

These types of problems are not limited to the construction industry. In fact, most industries are encountering these issues. All industries can benefit from this EQ methodology by focusing more on the human factor. When you get right down to it, business is all about people. And people are all about emotional intelligence. Let's put the people dimension back into our business. Let's make the phrase "people are our most important asset" more than just a slogan. Your employees are your only long-term, competitive advantage. Companies must pay attention to the people profit connection. Because if companies take care of their people, people will take care of their companies, and profits will soar.

Appendix A

Please visit my website for the following FREE resources:

Click on the download center, register and create a profile, and download away!

You will be able to access the following:

Case studies, which show the before and after EQ-i® group scores as well as individual comments from the participants.

A mini-emotional intelligence test. Note: this is not a validated test and should not be used for personal development. It may be used to indicate some areas that need improvement. You may also compare your profile to the typical construction manager profile.

El workbook, which will enable you to analyze your EQ-i® results and create a development plan. We include some resources for developing all of the 15 emotional competencies as measured by the Bar-On EQ-i®. This workbook is for individual use only. It is not to be copied for use by companies.

Basic meditation, breathing, and mindfulness techniques along with links to basic yoga postures, including desk yoga so that you can do yoga at your desk.

Many FREE articles and links to cool videos

Also available through my website:

Relationship Skills for Tough Guys: 12 Steps to Great Relationships

Stress Management, Time Management, and Life Balance for Tough Guys: Creating Success on Your Terms

Communication and Presentation Skills for Tough Guys

The Tao of Emotional Intelligence: 82 Ways to Improve Your Social Competence

The Primal Safety Coloring Book

Guided Mediation CD: Three music tracks and four guided meditations including progressive relaxation

Notes

1. How to Win Friends and Influence People by Dale Carnegie, Simon and Schuster Pocket Books, 1936.

2. Emotional Intelligence by Daniel Goleman, Bantam Books, 1995.

3. "Comment on R.J. Emmerling and Daniel Goleman, Emotional Intelligence: Issues and Common Misunderstandings" by David Caruso, PhD.

4. Source: National Institute for Occupational Safety and Health.

5. Working with Emotional Intelligence by Daniel Goleman, Bantam Books, 1998.

6. Source: World Almanac, 2004.

7. Work to Live: The Guide to Getting a Life by Joe Robinson, The Berkley Publishing Group, 2003.

8. Engineering News Record, July 19, 2004.

9. "Coaching the Alpha Male" by Kate Ludeman and Eddie Erlandson, Harvard Business Review, May 2004.

10. "Primal Leadership" by Daniel Goleman, Richard Boyatziz, and Annie McKee, Harvard Business Review, December 2001.

11. Joe Torre's Ground Rules for Winners by Joe Torre with Henry Dreher, Hyperion, 1999.

12. The Jobs Rated Almanac by Les Krantz, St. Martin's Press, 2005.

13. Baby Boomers are born between 1946 and 1964.
    Generation X are born between 1965 and 1980.

Generation Y are born between 1981 and 1999.

14. Source: FMI 2004–2005 Contractor Productivity Survey.

15. Source: National Academy of Sciences Task Force on Intellectual Property Management, September 1999.

16. Percentages of women's positions courtesy of NAWIC (National Association of Women in Construction)

17. Source: Annie R. Pearce, PhD., Program Director, Sustainable Facilties and Infrastructure Program, Georgia Institute of Technology, Atlanta, Georgia, USA.

18. Marilyn Elias, "Sunlight Reduces Need for Pain Medication", USA Today (March 2, 2004)

19. "Drain on the Bottom Line", Engineering News Record, May 8, 2006.

20. Working with Emotional Intelligence by Daniel Goleman, Bantam Books, 1998.

Biography and Contact Information

Brent Darnell is a leading authority on emotional intelligence and is a pioneer of its use in the construction industry. Brent has helped to improve the social competence of thousands of people working with over 70 companies in more than 15 countries around the world. There is constant demand for him to deliver speeches and train others using his comprehensive and unique approach that leads to lasting behavioral transformation.

An engineer, author, actor, playwright, and musician, Darnell gives presentations that are insightful, perceptive, and wildly entertaining. The construction industry has embraced his work, and many top companies like Clark, Granite, Kiewit, Caddell, Batson Cook, Brasfield & Gorrie, INPO, S&ME, Langan Engineers, Geotechnical Services, Inc, Pinkerton & Laws, Randall Paulson, Manhattan, Lyles, Newcomb & Boyd, Guarantee Electric, Hardin, McCarthy, Heery, Jacobsen, Cousins Properties, WS Nielsen, Balfour Beatty, and Skanska, have utilized his methods for their managers. He has also worked with the CMAA, the DBIA, ASFE, the Associated General Contractors, and the Associated Builders and Contractors. In addition, he is an adjunct professor at Penn State, Auburn and Virginia Tech, teaching people skills to their technical students.

Brent believes a person's emotional intelligence is one of the most important predictors of ultimate success for individuals and companies, and his proven program creates fundamental behavioral shifts in employees, improving their performance and increasing the company's bottom line. Brent is a graduate of the Georgia Institute of Technology, and lives in Atlanta, GA with his wife Andrea and their dog Ginger.

If you wish to contact Brent Darnell concerning this emotional intelligence work, please visit www.brentdarnell.com. Also check out the Total Leadership Program website at www.totalleadershipprogram.com .

You may also email him at *brent@brentdarnell.com*
or drop him a line at
Post Office Box 13064
Atlanta, GA 30324
USA